# THE ESSENTIAL NINJA CREAMI COOKBOOK FOR BEGINNERS

Discover New Ninja Creami Recipes for Delectable Ice Cream, Sorbet, Gelato, Milkshakes, Smoothie Bowls, Light Ice Cream, and Mix-in

Gertrude Ciotti

| | |
|---|---|
| Introduciton: | 5 |
| What is Ninja Creami | 6 |
| How it Works | 6 |
| Advantages of the Ninja Creami | 7 |
| User Guide of Ninja Creami? | 7 |
| How To Clean Ninja Creami Ice Cream Maker | 9 |
| Ninja Creami Maintenance Guides | 10 |

## NINJA CREAMI SORBETS ............................................................................................................. 11

| | |
|---|---|
| 1. NINJA CREAMI LEMON SORBET | 11 |
| 2. NINJA CREAMI MANGO SORBET | 12 |
| 3. SPIKED SELTZER SHERBET SHAKE | 13 |
| 4. NINJA CREAMI ORANGE SORBET | 14 |
| 5. NINJA CREAMI PEACH SORBET | 15 |
| 6. CREAMY PERSIMMON SORBET | 16 |
| 7. NINJA CREAMI PINA COLADA LIGHT SORBET | 17 |
| 8. APPLE CINNAMON SORBET | 18 |
| 9. BLUEBERRY LEMONADE SORBET | 19 |
| 10. BLUEBERRY LEMON SORBET | 20 |
| 11. CHERRY PIE SORBET | 21 |
| 12. CHILI LIME MANGO SORBET | 22 |
| 13. CHERRY SORBET | 23 |
| 14. DARK CHOCOLATE SORBET | 24 |
| 15. MIXED BERRY SORBET | 26 |
| 16. PINEAPPLE DOLE WHIP SORBET | 27 |
| 17. PLUM AMARETTO SORBET | 28 |
| 18. FROUNCEEN EGGNOG SORBET | 29 |
| 19. FRUIT PARADISE SORBET | 30 |
| 20. RASPBERRY PEACH SORBET | 31 |
| 21. RASPBERRY SORBET | 32 |

## NINJA CREAMI GALATO RECIPES ................................................................................................. 33

| | |
|---|---|
| 22. PUMPKIN PIE GELATO | 33 |
| 23. RICOTTA GELATO WITH PISTACHIO AND FIGS | 34 |
| 24. MAPLE GELATO | 36 |
| 25. NINJA CREAMI LEMON GELATO | 37 |
| 26. Ninja Creami Gelato Recipes (Limoncello Gelato) | 38 |
| 27. BLUEBERRY CHEESECAKE GELATO | 39 |
| 28. CHOCOLATE CHERRY STRACCIATELLA GELATO | 40 |
| 29. EGGNOG ICE CREAM GELATO | 42 |
| 30. PEACHES AND CREAM OATMEAL GELATO | 43 |
| 31. NINJA CREAMI PEPPERMINT STICK GELATO | 44 |
| 32. BROWNIE BATTER GELATO | 46 |
| 33. BUTTER PECAN GELATO | 47 |
| 34. BLACK CHERRY GELATO | 49 |
| 35. EGGNOG GELATO | 50 |

## NINJA CREAMI ICE CREAM MIX - INS ........................................................................................... 51

| | |
|---|---|
| 36. S'MORES ICE CREAM | 51 |
| 37. RASPBERRY WHITE TRUFFLE ICE CREAM | 53 |
| 38. FROUNCEEN HOT CHOCOLATE ICE CREAM | 55 |

- 39. BANANA CHOCOLATE CHIP LITE ICE CREAM .................................................................................. 56
- 40. COPYCAT CHUNKY MONKEY ICE CREAM .................................................................................... 57
- 41. CHOCOLATE PEANUT BUTTER BANANA ICE CREAM .................................................................... 58
- 42. Mint Chocolate Ice Cream ........................................................................................................... 59
- 43. NINJA CREAMI PINA COLADA LIGHT ICE CREAM ......................................................................... 60
- 44. BANANA PUDDING ICE CREAM ................................................................................................... 61
- 45. BLUEBERRY PIE ICE CREAM ......................................................................................................... 62
- 46. BOOUNCEY CHERRY GARCIA ICE CREAM .................................................................................... 64
- 47. BUTTER PECAN ICE CREAM ......................................................................................................... 65
- 48. CHOCOLATE CHIP ICE CREAM ..................................................................................................... 66
- 49. CHOCOLATE PEANUT BUTTER BANANA ICE CREAM .................................................................... 67
- 50. COOKIES AND CREAM ICE CREAM ............................................................................................... 68

## NINJA CREMI ICE CREAM .................................................................................................................. 69

- 51. Peanut Butter Ice Cream .............................................................................................................. 69
- 52. Italian Crema Ice Cream ............................................................................................................... 70
- 53. Keto Peanut Butter Cup ofIce Cream ........................................................................................... 71
- 54. Ninja Creami Key Lime Pie Ice Cream .......................................................................................... 72
- 55. NINJA CREAMI LEMON COOKIE ICE CREAM ................................................................................ 74
- 56. NINJA CREAMI MEXICAN HOT CHOCOLATE ICE CREAM .............................................................. 75
- 57. NINJA CREAMI MINT CHOCOLATE CHIP ICE CREAM .................................................................... 76
- 58. MULLED APPLE CIDER ICE CREAM ............................................................................................... 77
- 59. Orange Creamsicle Ice Cream ...................................................................................................... 79
- 60. PEACH COBBLER FROUNCEEN YOGURT ...................................................................................... 80
- 61. NINJA CREAMI PEACH ICE CREAM ............................................................................................... 81
- 62. APPLE PIE ICE CREAM .................................................................................................................. 82
- 63. BANANA ICE CREAM ................................................................................................................... 84
- 64. BANANA SWEET CREAM ICE CREAM ........................................................................................... 85
- 65. Ninja Creami Salted Caramel Ice Cream ...................................................................................... 86
- 66. CARAMEL MOCHA OREO CRUMBLE ICE CREAM ......................................................................... 88
- 67. CHOCOLATE ICE CREAM .............................................................................................................. 89
- 68. CINNAMON SPICE FROUNCEEN YOGURT-LITE ICE CREAM .......................................................... 90
- 69. COCONUT LIME ICE CREAM ........................................................................................................ 91
- 70. COFFEE ICE CREAM ..................................................................................................................... 92
- 71. DAIRY-FREE PUMPKIN ICE CREAM .............................................................................................. 93
- 72. FROUNCEEN YOGURT ice Cream ................................................................................................. 94
- 73. PISTACHIO ICE *CREAM* .............................................................................................................. 95
- 74. PROTEIN ICE CREAM ................................................................................................................... 96
- 75. PUMPKIN ICE CREAM .................................................................................................................. 97

## NINJA CREAMI MILK SHAKE ............................................................................................................... 98

- 76. VEGAN PEANUT BUTTER COOKIE MILKSHAKE ............................................................................. 98
- 77. NINJA CREAMI LOW CALORIE CHOCOLATE CHEESECAKE ............................................................ 99
- 78. STRAWBERRY BANANA MILKSHAKE .......................................................................................... 100
- 79. THICK CHOCOLATE MILKSHAKE ................................................................................................. 101
- 80. VANILLA MILKSHAKE ................................................................................................................. 102
- 81. DAIRY-FREE TAHINI CHOCOLATE COFFEE MILKSHAKE ............................................................... 103
- 82. COFFEE AND CREAM MILKSHAKE .............................................................................................. 104
- 83. ALMOND CANDY BAR MILKSHAKE ............................................................................................ 105

## NINJA SMOOTHIE BOWLS ................................................................................................................ 106

84. ALOHA TROPICAL SMOOTHIE bowl......106
85. BLUEBERRY MUFFIN SMOOTHIE BOWL......107
86. PITAYA PINEAPPLE SMOOTHIE BOWL......108
87. PINEAPPLE CUCUMBER SMOOTHIE BOWL......109
88. WATERMELON SMOOTHIE BOWL......110
89. GLOWING GREEN SMOOTHIE BOWL......111
90. HEALTHY STRAWBERRY BANANA SMOOTHIE BOWL......112
91. STRAWBERRY BANANA PROTEIN SMOOTHIE BOWL......113
92. Ninja cremi RAZZLEBERRY SMOOTHIE BOWL......114
93. BANANA PEANUT BUTTER OAT BOWL......115
94. AVOCADO KALE SMOOTHIE BOWL......117
95. NINJA CREAMI COFFEE SMOOTHIE BOWL......116

# INTRODUCITON:

Welcome to "The Essential Ninja Creami Cookbook for Beginners"! This cookbook is the result of a passionate journey to bring the joy and satisfaction of creating homemade frounceen desserts to your kitchen, using the innovative Ninja Creami machine. With this book, you will embark on an exciting culinary adventure, discovering new recipes and techniques that will elevate your dessert-making skills and delight your taste buds.

When I first encountered the Ninja Creami machine, I was amazed by its versatility and ease of use. This remarkable device has revolutionized the way we create frounceen treats at home, and I wanted to share my passion for this appliance with others. That's when the idea of this cookbook was born. My goal was to create a user-friendly guide for beginners, filled with scrumptious recipes and helpful tips to make the most of your Ninja Creami experience.

In this book, you will find a diverse collection of recipes, ranging from traditional favorites to innovative flavor combinations. We have carefully curated recipes for classic ice creams, sorbets, and gelatos, as well as delicious milkshakes, nourishing smoothie bowls, and lighter ice cream options for those watching their calorie intake. Additionally, we have included exciting mix-ins to personalize your creations and add an extra touch of creativity to your desserts.

As you explore the pages of this cookbook, you will learn the essentials of using the Ninja Creami machine, as well as valuable tips and tricks to ensure consistent, high-quality results every time. We have taken special care to provide clear, step-by-step instructions and ingredient lists in each recipe, making it easy for beginners to follow and succeed in their dessert-making endeavors.

"The Essential Ninja Creami Cookbook for Beginners" is more than just a collection of recipes; it is an invitation to join a community of fellow dessert lovers who share a common passion for creating delightful frounceen treats. By using this cookbook, you will not only enhance your culinary skills but also create lasting memories with friends and family as you enjoy the delicious desserts you've crafted together.

So, let's embark on this sweet journey together. Grab your Ninja Creami machine, gather your ingredients, and prepare to experience the magic of homemade frounceen treats. Here's to delectable, satisfying, and unforgettable dessert moments with "The Essential Ninja Creami Cookbook for Beginners"!

**With warmest regards,**

"Gertrude Ciotti"

## WHAT IS NINJA CREAMI

The Ninja Creami is a versatile kitchen appliance developed by Ninja, a brand known for its innovative home and kitchen products. The full name of the device is the Ninja CREAMi Ice Cream, Gelato, and Sorbet Maker. As the name suggests, the Creami is designed to create various frounceen treats, including ice cream, gelato, sorbet, milkshakes, and more, all from the comfort of your home.

## HOW IT WORKS

The Ninja Creami works by using a patented technology called "Creamify" that transforms frounceen ingredients into a smooth, creamy texture. The process involves three main steps:

**Prep:** You'll need to blend your desired ingredients, such as fruits, milk, cream, or other flavorings, and then freeze the mixture in a specially designed pint container. This container should be frounceen for at least 24 hours before use.

**Creamify:** Once the ingredients are frounceen, you'll place the pint container into the Creami machine. The Creami will then use a combination of its motor and unique scraper system to break down and churn the frounceen ingredients, creating a smooth and creamy texture.

**Customize:** Depending on your preferences, you can choose from different settings on the machine, such as ice cream, gelato, or sorbet, which will produce different textures and consistencies. You can also add mix-ins or toppings to further personalize your frounceen treat.

## ADVANTAGES OF THE NINJA CREAMI

**Versatility:** The Creami offers a wide range of frounceen treat options, allowing you to make various desserts according to your taste preferences and dietary needs.

**Customization:** With the ability to choose your ingredients, mix-ins, and settings, the Creami provides a highly customizable experience, catering to individual tastes and dietary restrictions.

**Freshness and quality:** Since you're making the frounceen treats yourself, you can ensure that the ingredients are fresh and of high quality. This also allows you to avoid preservatives and artificial ingredients commonly found in store-bought ice cream.

**Easy cleanup:** The Creami is designed to be easy to clean, with dishwasher-safe parts and a compact design for easy storage.

In conclusion, the Ninja Creami is an innovative kitchen appliance that allows you to create a variety of frounceen treats, such as ice cream, gelato, and sorbet, at home. With its customizable features, easy cleanup, and versatility, it's a great addition to any kitchen for those who love to experiment with different frounceen dessert recipes.

## USER GUIDE OF NINJA CREAMI?

A comprehensive user guide should come with your Ninja Creami upon purchase. However, here's a basic overview of how to use the device:

**Assemble the Ninja Creami:**

- Place the base unit on a stable, flat surface.
- Attach the motor assembly on top of the base unit by aligning the arrows and pressing down until it clicks into place.
- Make sure the power cord is plugged into an electrical outlet.

**Prepare the ingredients:**

- Choose a recipe, either from the Ninja Creami recipe book, the Ninja Kitchen website, or create your own.
- Blend the ingredients together as required by the recipe.
- Pour the blended mixture into the provided pint container.
- Place the pint container in the freezer for at least 24 hours to ensure it is fully frounceen.

**Creamify your frounceen treat:**

- Remove the frounceen pint container from the freezer.
- Place the frounceen pint into the motor assembly of the Ninja Creami.
- Attach the lid to the pint container and turn it clockwise to secure it.
- Choose the desired program on the control panel (ice cream, gelato, sorbet, etc.) and press the "Start" button.
- The Ninja Creami will automatically begin the Creamify process, breaking down the frounceen mixture and turning it into a smooth, creamy treat.

**Customize your treat (optional):**

- If you'd like to add mix-ins, pause the machine using the "Pause" button, open the lid, and add your desired mix-ins.
- Close the lid and press the "Start" button to resume the Creamify process.

**Serve and enjoy:**

- Once the Creamify process is complete, the machine will beep to let you know it's done.
- Remove the lid and use the provided scraper to scoop out your frounceen treat.
- Serve immediately for a soft-serve texture, or transfer the treat to an airtight container and freeze it for a firmer texture.

Remember to consult the user guide provided with your Ninja Creami for more detailed instructions, troubleshooting tips, and safety information. Enjoy experimenting with different recipes and creating your own delicious frounceen treats!

## HOW TO CLEAN NINJA CREAMI ICE CREAM MAKER

Cleaning the Ninja Creami ice cream maker is relatively simple and straightforward. Here are the steps to clean the appliance:

**Turn off and unplug:** After using the Ninja Creami, ensure that the appliance is turned off, and unplug it from the electrical outlet.

**Disassemble:** Remove the motor assembly from the base unit by lifting it up. Remove the pint container, lid, and scraper.

**Clean removable parts:** Wash the pint container, lid, and scraper with warm, soapy water. Alternatively, you can place these parts in the dishwasher, as they are dishwasher-safe. Rinse thoroughly and let them air dry or use a soft, clean cloth to dry them.

**Clean the base unit and motor assembly:** Do NOT submerge the base unit or motor assembly in water or place them in the dishwasher, as this may damage the electrical components. Instead, use a damp cloth or sponge to gently wipe down the exterior of the base unit and motor assembly. Make sure to remove any residue or spills. Dry the surfaces with a clean, soft cloth.

**Reassemble:** Once all the parts are clean and dry, you can reassemble the Ninja Creami by placing the motor assembly back onto the base unit. Store the pint container, lid, and scraper in a clean, dry place until the next use.

For optimal performance and to maintain the appliance's longevity, clean the Ninja Creami after each use. Always consult the user guide provided with your device for specific cleaning instructions and safety information.

# NINJA CREAMI MAINTENANCE GUIDES

Proper maintenance of your Ninja Creami ice cream maker is essential to ensure its longevity and optimal performance. Here's a general maintenance guide to help you keep your appliance in good working condition:

**Regular cleaning:** Clean your Ninja Creami after each use, following the cleaning instructions mentioned in a previous response. Regular cleaning will prevent the buildup of residue and bacteria, ensuring the appliance remains hygienic and functions well.

**Inspect parts for wear or damage:** Periodically examine the removable parts (pint container, lid, and scraper) for any signs of wear, damage, or cracks. If you notice any issues, replace the damaged parts to ensure proper functioning and to prevent any contamination of your frounceen treats.

**Store in a cool, dry place:** When not in use, store the Ninja Creami and its components in a cool, dry place away from direct sunlight and heat sources. This will help preserve the appliance's materials and prevent any potential warping or damage.

**Avoid overloading:** Do not overfill the pint container or add too many mix-ins during the Creamify process, as this can put excessive strain on the motor and cause damage or malfunction. Always follow the recommended guidelines provided in the user guide or recipe book.

**Check the power cord and plug:** Periodically inspect the power cord and plug for any signs of wear, damage, or fraying. If you notice any issues, discontinue use and contact Ninja customer support for assistance or replacement.

**Keep the user guide handy:** Retain the user guide that comes with your Ninja Creami and refer to it for specific maintenance instructions, troubleshooting tips, and safety information.

By following these maintenance tips and adhering to the user guide's recommendations, you can help ensure your Ninja Creami ice cream maker remains in good working condition and provides you with delicious frounceen treats for years to come.

# NINJA CREAMI SORBETS

## 1. NINJA CREAMI LEMON SORBET

Prep Time: 5 minutes

Freeze time: 1 day

Total Time: 1 DAY 5 Mins

Serving: 4

### Ingredients

- 1/4 cup of monk fruit sweetener
- 1/2 cup of lemon juice
- 1 Tbsp raw agave nectar (optional)
- 1 cup of warm water

### Instructions

1. In a small bowl, mix together the warm water, monk fruit sweetener, and raw agave nectar (if using) until the sweetener is completely dissolved.
2. Add the fresh lemon juice to the mixture and stir until well combined.
3. Pour the mixture into a CREAMi pint, taking care not to exceed the MAX FILL line. Securely place the lid onto the pint.
4. Freeze the pint for 24 hours.
5. Remove the pint from the freezer and place it into the outer bowl of the Ninja CREAMi machine.
6. Attach the paddle to the lid and install the lid onto the outer bowl.
7. Plug in the Ninja CREAMi machine and then install the bowl onto the base.
8. Press the power button and select LITE ICE CREAM.
9. When the machine shuts off, carefully remove the bowl from the base and take off the lid.
10. If the sorbet is crumbly, reattach the lid and install the bowl onto the base again. Select RE-SPIN. Repeat this step up to two times if necessary.
11. Once the sorbet is at the right consistency, serve it immediately.

## 2. NINJA CREAMI MANGO SORBET

Prep Time: 5 Mins

Freeze Time : 1 Day

Spin Time: 3 Mins

Total Time: 1 Day 8 Mins

Serving: 4

### Ingredients

- 16 ounce. frounceen mango slices, THAWED
- 2 TBSP monk fruit sweetener (optional)

### Instructions

1. If using monk fruit sweetener, mix it with thawed mango slices in a medium bowl. Stir until the sweetener is evenly distributed over the mango slices and is beginning to dissolve.
2. Pour the mango slices into a CREAMi pint, packing the slices together as you fill the pint. Ensure that there are no gaps between slices, and they don't go over the MAX FILL line. Put the lid on it.
3. Place the pint in the freezer and freeze for 24 hours. Ensure that it's level.
4. Take the pint from the freezer, remove the lid, and place it in the outer bowl of the Ninja CREAMi. Install the paddle in the lid and attach the lid to the outer bowl.
5. Plug in the Ninja CREAMi unit and install the bowl on the base.
6. Press the power button and select SORBET.
7. When the unit shuts off, remove the bowl from the base and remove the lid.
8. If the sorbet is crumbly, reattach the lid and install the bowl on the base again. Select RE-SPIN. You can re-spin the mixture twice if needed.
9. Once the sorbet is at the right consistency, serve immediately. Enjoy!

## 3. SPIKED SELTZER SHERBET SHAKE

Prep Time: 5 minutes

Total Time: 7 minutes

Serving: 1

### *Ingredients*

- 1/2 cup of TRULY Lime Seltzer
- 1 1/2 cups of store-bought rainbow sherbet

### *Instructions*

1. Take an empty CREAMi™ Pint and add the rainbow sherbet and TRULY Lime Seltzer to it, in the order listed.
2. Put the pint inside the outer bowl and affix the Creamerizer™ paddle onto the lid of the outer bowl.
3. Secure the lid assembly onto the outer bowl, and position the bowl assembly onto the motor base.
4. Turn the handle in a rightward direction to lift the platform and lock it firmly in position.
5. Choose the MILKSHAKE setting on the device.
6. After the processing is done, take out the milkshake from the pint and serve right away.

## 4. NINJA CREAMI ORANGE SORBET

Prep Time: 5 Minutes

Freeze Time: 1 Day

Spin Time: 3 Mins

Total Time: 1 Day 8 Minutes

Serving: 4

### *Ingredients*

- 20 ounce canned mandarin orange slices in their own juice
- 2 TBSP monk fruit sweetener (optional)

### *Instructions*

1. If you are using monk fruit sweetener, combine it with the mandarin orange slices and their juice in a medium bowl. Stir the mixture until the sweetener dissolves completely.
2. Next, pour the mandarin orange mixture into a pint-sized CREAMi container, being careful not to fill it above the MAX FILL line. If you accidentally pour too much, remove enough juice to bring the level below the line before putting the lid on.
3. Place the container in the freezer, making sure it is level, and allow it to freeze for 24 hours.
4. After 24 hours, take the container out of the freezer, remove the lid, and place it in the outer bowl of the Ninja CREAMi. Attach the paddle to the lid and secure it onto the outer bowl.
5. Plug in the Ninja CREAMi and put the bowl on the base. Select the SORBET option on the power button.
6. When the unit shuts off, remove the bowl from the base and take off the lid. If the sorbet appears crumbly, attach the lid again and place the bowl on the base. Choose the RE-SPIN option. You can repeat this step up to two times until the sorbet reaches the right consistency.
7. Once the sorbet has the desired texture, serve it immediately.

## 5. NINJA CREAMI PEACH SORBET

Prep Time: 5 Minutes

Freeze Time: 1 Day

Total Time: 1 Day 5 Minutes

Serving: 1

### Ingredients

- 15.25 Ounces Peaches (Canned- Chunks)

### Instructions

1. Pour the canned peaches, including the liquid, into a Ninja Creami pint container. Freeze the container on a level surface in a cold freezer for a full 24 hours.
2. After 24 hours, remove the pint from the freezer and take off the lid.
3. Place the Ninja Creami pint into the outer bowl and insert it into the Ninja Creami machine. Turn the outer bowl until it locks into place.
4. Press the SORBET button and let the machine mix the sorbet until it becomes very creamy. This should take about 2 minutes.
5. Once the SORBET function has ended, twist the outer bowl and release it from the machine.
6. If the sorbet is not creamy enough, place the outer bowl with the pint back into the Ninja Creami machine and lock it into place. Choose the RE-SPIN function. Once the Ninja Creami completes the RE-SPIN cycle, remove the outer bowl from the machine.
7. Your canned peach sorbet is now ready to eat! Enjoy!

# 6. CREAMY PERSIMMON SORBET

Prep Time: 20 Mins

Freeze Time: 2 Hrs

Total Time: 2 Hrs 20 mins

Serving: 1

## Ingredients

- 4 ripe persimmons
- 1 cup of heavy cream
- 1/2 cups of sugar
- 1/4 cup of water
- 1 tbsp lemon juice

## Instructions

1. Cut the persimmons into small pieces, removing any seeds or tough parts.
2. In a saucepan, combine the sugar and water and bring to a boil over medium heat. Stir until the sugar dissolves completely, then remove from heat and let cool.
3. In a food processor, pure the persimmons until they are smooth.
4. Add the cooled sugar syrup, heavy cream, and lemon juice to the blender and blend until everything is combined.
5. Pour the mixture into a container and place it in the freezer for at least 4 hours. Every hour or so, take the container out of the freezer and stir the mixture to break up any ice crystals that have formed.
6. When ready to serve, let the sorbet sit at room temperature for a few minutes to soften slightly. Then scoop into bowls or cones and enjoy!

## 7. NINJA CREAMI PINA COLADA LIGHT SORBET

Prep Time: 5 Min

Freeze Time: 1 Day

Total Time: 1 Day 5 Min

Serving: 1

### *Ingredients*

- ¼ Cup of Almond Milk Creamer
- 15 Ounce Sliced Pineapple
- 3 Tbsp Coco Lopez or Coco Real
- 1 Tbsp Coconut

### *Instructions*

1. To make delicious sorbet, begin by pouring all the necessary Ingredients (excluding the shredded coconut) into the pint container and stir them together. Smooth the mixture out and cover it before freezing it for 24 hours.
2. Once you are ready to proceed, remove the container from the freezer and allow it to sit at room temperature for 10 minutes. Then, place the pint container into the outer bowl and insert it into the Ninja Creami machine.
3. Turn the machine on and choose the sorbet process. Allow the machine to spin the mixture using the sorbet process until it becomes smooth and creamy.
4. If you want to add shredded coconut to your sorbet, you can do so in two ways. First, you can simply remove the sorbet from the machine and sprinkle the coconut on top before enjoying. Alternatively, you can create a small tunnel down the middle of the sorbet and add the coconut as a mix-in.
5. If you choose to add the coconut as a mix-in, place the pint container back into the outer bowl and into the Ninja Creami machine. Select the mix-ins function and wait until the process is complete.
6. Finally, scoop out the sorbet and enjoy!

## 8. APPLE CINNAMON SORBET

Prep Time: 5 minutes

Cook Time: 2 minutes

Additional Time: 1 day

Total Time: 1 day 7 minutes

Serving: 4

### *Ingredients*

- 1 can (21 ounce) of apple pie filling

### *Instructions*

1. Scoop the apple pie filling into a pint-sized container, such as the Ninja Creami pint. Be careful not to go over the maximum fill line. Use a spoon to smooth out the top as much as possible.
2. Close the container with a lid and place it on a level surface in the freezer. Allow it to freeze for at least 24 hours.
3. After 24 hours, remove the container from the freezer and take off the lid. Place the container in the outer bowl and secure the lid.
4. Lock the bowl apparatus into the Ninja Creami machine.
5. Press the Sorbet button on the machine and let it run its cycle, which should take approximately 2 minutes.
6. Once the cycle is complete, remove the bowl apparatus from the Ninja Creami machine.
7. Scoop the sorbet into serving dishes and enjoy your delicious homemade apple pie sorbet!

## 9. BLUEBERRY LEMONADE SORBET

Prep Time: 5 minutes

Cook Time: 2 minutes

Additional Time: 1 day

Total Time: 1 day 7 minutes

Serving: 1 pint

### Ingredients

- 2/3 cup of fresh blueberries
- 1 1/3 cups of pink or yellow lemonade
- 1/4 cup of whole milk
- 1 tbsp of soft cream cheese

### Instructions

1. In a bowl, mix the softened cream cheese and milk by hand until you have a smooth consistency. Alternatively, you can use a small blender or food processor.
2. Add the lemonade and blueberries to the milk mixture, and stir to combine.
3. Pour the mixture into a Ninja Creami pint container, and close the lid tightly. Transfer the container to a level surface in your freezer, and freeze it for 24 hours.
4. After 24 hours, remove the container from the freezer and take off the lid. Place the pint container in the outer bowl of the Ninja Creami, and attach the outer bowl lid.
5. Secure the outer bowl into the Ninja Creami machine, and press the Sorbet button. Allow the cycle to run for about 2 minutes.
6. Take out the outer bowl from the machine and check the texture of the sorbet. If it appears crumbly, add a tbsp of milk, and put the outer bowl back into the machine for a Re-spin cycle. Repeat this step as needed until you achieve the desired texture.

# 10. BLUEBERRY LEMON SORBET

Prep Time: 5 minutes

Freeze Time: 1 day

Total Time: 1 day 5 minutes

Serving: 1 pint

## *Ingredients*

- 1 1/2 cup of lemonade
- 1/4 cup of milk
- 1/3 cup of blueberries, fresh or frounceen
- 1 tbsp cream cheese, room temperature or microwave for 10-20 seconds

## *Instructions*

1. Start Mixing together in a medium Size bowl softened cream cheese and milk until well combined. It's okay if there are some small chunks of cream cheese.
2. Add the lemonade to the bowl and mix well.
3. Pour the mixture into a Ninja Creami pint container and add the blueberries. Freeze on a level surface in a cold freezer for 24 hours.
4. After 24 hours, remove the pint from the freezer and take off the lid.
5. Place the Ninja Creami pint into the outer bowl and lock it into place. Insert the outer bowl with the pint into the Ninja Creami machine and turn it until the outer bowl is locked in.
6. Press the SORBET button and let the machine run for about 2 minutes. During this time, the sorbet will mix together and become creamy.
7. Once the SORBET function is complete, turn the outer bowl and remove it from the machine.
8. Enjoy your sorbet immediately! If the sorbet isn't creamy enough, place the outer bowl back into the machine and use the RE-SPIN function. Once the cycle is complete, remove the bowl from the machine and enjoy.

## 11. CHERRY PIE SORBET

Prep Time: 5 minutes

Cook Time: 2 minutes

Additional Time: 1 day

Total Time: 1 day 7 minutes

Serving: 1 pint

### *Ingredients*

- 21-ounce of cherry pie filling
- Optional: 1/4 cup of chopped graham crackers for mixing in or topping

### *Instructions*

1. Scoop the cherry pie filling into the Ninja Creami pint, making sure not to exceed the max fill line. Use a spoon to smooth the top down as much as possible.
2. Close the lid and transfer the pint to a level surface in your freezer. Freeze it for at least 24 hours.
3. After 24 hours, remove the pint from the freezer and take off the lid.
4. Place the pint in the outer bowl of the Ninja Creami machine and secure the outer bowl lid. Lock the bowl apparatus into the machine.
5. Press the Sorbet button and let the cycle run for about 2 minutes.
6. When the cycle is complete, remove the bowl apparatus from the Ninja Creami machine.
7. If you want to add mix-ins, create a well in the sorbet that's about 1/2-inch wide and extends to the bottom of the container. Add 1/4 cup of chopped graham crackers to the well and run the pint through the Mix-in cycle. Alternatively, you can top each serving of sorbet with chopped graham crackers or omit the graham crackers altogether.
8. Serve and enjoy your homemade cherry pie sorbet!

## 12. CHILI LIME MANGO SORBET

Prep Time: 10 minutes

Freeze Time: 8 hours

Total Time: 8 hours 10 minutes

Serving: 4

### *Ingredients*

- 1/2 cup of canned full-fat coconut milk
- 2 tbsp maple syrup
- Juice and zest one large lime
- 3 cup of frounceen mango
- 1-2 tsp chili lime seasoning

### *Instructions*

1. Place all Ingredients in a high-speed blender or food processor and blend until completely smooth. If using a blender with a tamper, use it to help blend all of the frounceen fruit.
2. If using a food processor, scrape down the sides as needed while processing until smooth.
3. Pour the mixture into a loaf pan and sprinkle with coconut flakes and extra spice, if desired.
4. Place the pan in the freezer, covered with foil.
5. Freeze for several hours or overnight until firm.

## 13. CHERRY SORBET

Prep Time: 2 minutes

Cook Time: 8 minutes

Freeze Time: 6-7 hours

Total Time: 6-7 hours 10 minutes

Serving: 6

### *Ingredients*

- 500g frounceen pitted cherries
- 125g caster sugar
- 1-2 tsp fresh lemon juice, to taste (see notes)

### *Instructions*

1. In a food processor bowl, combine the frounceen cherries and caster sugar. Process the mixture until it is smooth, and scrape down the sides of the bowl as needed.
2. Once the mixture is smooth, add 1-2 tsp of fresh lemon juice to taste.
3. Pour the mixture into a container and freeze for 6-7 hours or until it is firm.
4. After the sorbet is frounceen, use an ice cream scoop or spoon to serve. Enjoy!
5. Note: Adjust the amount of lemon juice to your liking, as the amount needed can vary depending on the sweetness of the cherries used.

## 14. DARK CHOCOLATE SORBET

Prep Time: 15 minutes

Cook Time: 20 minutes

Freeze Time: 11 hours

Total Time: 11 hours 35 minutes

Serving: 10

### Ingredients

- Sea salt to sprinkle
- 1 ¼ cup of brewed espresso
- ⅓ – ½ cup ofc oconut sugar or raw sugar
- 1 tsp pure vanilla extract or chocolate extract
- ⅓ – ½ cup of maple syrup
- 2 Tbsp intense unsweetened cocoa powder
- 1 ¾ – 2 cups of dark chocolate chips (for the vegan option, use Enjoy Life)
- 4 cups of purified water
- Optional: melted dark chocolate and crushed nuts of choice

### Instructions

1. In a small pot, combine the brewed espresso, sugar, water, vanilla/chocolate extract, and maple syrup. Bring to a boil and then reduce to medium heat. Stir for about 15-17 minutes until the coffee/sugar mixture thickens. It won't caramelize, but it will turn into a thicker texture, almost like syrup. Remove from heat and set aside.
2. In the other bowl combine the cocoa powder and chocolate chips. Add a pinch of sea salt if desired. Pour in the hot coffee/sugar mixture and whisk everything together until the chocolate is melted and combined with the coffee.

3. Pour the mixture into a tin lined with parchment paper. Add a few tbsp of coffee or espresso beans on top, if desired. Place in the freezer for at least 8 hours.
4. Once the coffee-chocolate mixture is frounceen, cut or break it into smaller pieces. This is to make it easier to blend.
5. Place the chocolate espresso pieces in a food processor or blender. Blend until a smooth texture has formed. This usually takes a few minutes.
6. Once smooth, use a spatula to place the smooth mixture back in a medium-sized lined canister or square tin.
7. Let it freeze again for another 2-3 hours.
8. When ready to serve, remove the canister from the freezer and let it sit for 5 minutes to thaw. Then, use an ice cream scooper to scoop the sorbet into bowls or onto a cone.
9. Drizzle melted dark chocolate and crushed nuts on top if desired.

## 15. MIXED BERRY SORBET

Prep Time: 10 minutes

Freeze Time: 1 day

Total Time: 1 day 10 minutes

Serving: 4

### Ingredients

- 1 cup of blueberries
- 1 cup of strawberries, stemmed and quartered
- 1 cup of raspberries

### Instructions

1. Pour the mixed fruit into an empty CREAMi™ Pint until it reaches the MAX FILL line.
2. Use a heavy kitchen utensil like a ladle or potato masher to firmly press the berries below the MAX FILL line. This will create a compact and even mixture that will make space for more berries.
3. Continue adding more berries and pressing down with the utensil until all the berries are packed tightly into the pint, just below the MAX FILL line. Then, cover the pint with the storage lid and place it in the freezer for 24 hours.
4. After 24 hours, remove the pint from the freezer and take off the lid. Put the pint in an outer bowl and attach the Creamerizer™ Paddle to the outer bowl lid. Lock the lid assembly onto the outer bowl and place the bowl assembly onto the motor base. Twist the handle to the right to raise the platform and lock it in place.
5. Choose the SORBET option on the motor base.
6. When the processing is complete, you can either add any mix-ins you want or remove the sorbet from the pint and serve it immediately. Enjoy your delicious homemade sorbet!

## 16. PINEAPPLE DOLE WHIP SORBET

Prep Time: 5 minutes

Freeze Time: 1 day 5 minutes

Total Time: 1 day 10 minutes

Serving: 2

### *Ingredients*

- 1/4 cup of non-dairy milk, as needed after the first spin
- 2 cups of canned or fresh pineapple in juice

### *Instructions*

1. Blend the pineapple and its juice in a blender until smooth, or simply dump the crushed pineapple or chunks straight into a Creami pint.
2. Do not fill the pint above the maximum fill line, and ensure the top is smooth and even. Place the pint on a level spot in the freezer and freeze for 24 hours.
3. Remove the lid from the pint and place it into the outer bowl base.
4. Insert the creamier blade into the outer lid.
5. Snap the outer lid onto the outer bowl, ensuring it locks securely.
6. Place the Creami with the handle pointing towards the front, and turn it to the right until the platform rises and the container locks in place. If it doesn't lock, you won't be able to turn it on.
7. Press the on button and churn the sorbet.
8. If the sorbet is crumbly, add a few tbsp of non-dairy milk and churn again using the re-spin button.
9. Depending on the temperature of your freezer, you may need to re-spin the sorbet again.

# 17. PLUM AMARETTO SORBET

Prep Time: 10 minutes

Freeze Time: 2-4 hours

Total Time: 2-4 hours 10 minutes

Serving: 8-10

## *Ingredients*

- 2 tsp of honey
- 2 tbsp of Amaretto
- 2 pounds (931 grams) of fresh plums

## *Instructions*

1. Prepare the plums by washing, pitting, and chopping them, leaving the skin intact.
2. Place the chopped plums in a blender or food processor and puree them until they are smooth.
3. Then, add the Amaretto and honey and blend again until the Ingredients are thoroughly mixed. Taste the mixture and make any necessary adjustments to the flavor.
4. If you have the time, chill the puree in the refrigerator until it becomes cold.
5. However, if you are eager to proceed, transfer the mixture into an ice cream maker and process it according to the instructions provided by the manufacturer. This typically takes around 20-30 minutes.
6. When the sorbet achieves a soft and creamy consistency, spoon it into an ice cream container or loaf pan of your choosing.
7. Freeze for a minimum of 2-4 hours or until the sorbet becomes perfectly scoopable.
8. Your homemade plum Amaretto sorbet is now ready to be served and enjoyed!

## 18. FROUNCEEN EGGNOG SORBET

Prep Time: 5 minutes

Freeze Time: 1 day

Total Time: 1 day 5 minutes

Serving: 4

### Ingredients

- 1 container (32 ounces) Hood® Golden Eggnog

### Instructions

1. Fill an empty CREAMi™ Pint up to the MAX FILL line by pouring in the Hood® Golden Eggnog, noting that the entire container may not be necessary.
2. After filling, cover the pint with the storage lid and freeze it for 24 hours.
3. Take the frounceen pint out of the freezer and remove the lid. Place the pint into an outer bowl and attach the Creamerizer Paddle to the lid of the outer bowl.
4. Lock the lid assembly onto the outer bowl and place the bowl assembly onto the motor base. Raise the platform and lock it in place by turning the handle to the right.
5. Select the SORBET option on the motor base.
6. When the processing is complete, take the Frounceen Eggnog out of the pint and serve it right away.
7. Enjoy your homemade Eggnog Sorbet, which is both creamy and delicious!

## 19. FRUIT PARADISE SORBET

Prep Time: 10 minutes

Freeze Time: 1 day

Total Time: 1 day 10 minutes

Serving: 3 pint

### *Ingredients*

- 15 ounces canned mandarin orange slices, including juice
- 2 small bananas
- 20 ounces of canned diced or cubed pineapple, including juice
- 15 ounces of canned red grapefruit sections, including juice
- optional: 1 tbsp maraschino cherries

### *Instructions*

1. In a large bowl, combine the canned pineapple, grapefruit sections, and mandarin orange slices, including their juices.
2. Peel and slice the bananas, and add them to the bowl of fruit.
3. Use a potato masher to mash the bananas into the fruit until the mixture is relatively smooth.
4. Mix the fruit and bananas together until well combined.
5. Pour the mixture into a pint-sized container up to the max fill line, and put the lid on.
6. If you have extra mixture, pour it into a deep baking pan and freeze it separately.
7. Freeze the pint-sized container of mixture for 24 hours.
8. After 24 hours, remove the pint container from the freezer and take off the lid.
9. Place the pint container in the outer bowl of your Ninja Creami machine and select the "Sorbet" function.
10. Once the machine has completed the sorbet function, remove the pint container and serve.

Optional: After processing the sorbet, remove the pint container and use a spoon to make a well in the center of the sorbet. Add maraschino cherries, and spin on mix-ins.If you frouncee any extra mixture in a baking pan, thaw it slightly and serve from the pan.

## 20. RASPBERRY PEACH SORBET

Prep Time: 5 minutes

Freeze Time: 5 hours

Total Time: 5 hours 5 minutes

Serving: 4

### Ingredients

- 1/2 tsp of lime juice
- 1 tsp of honey
- 1/4 cup of freshly squeezed orange juice
- 1/4 cup of pineapple chunks with natural juice (without added sugar)
- 1 cup of fresh raspberries
- 3 cups of sliced and peeled peaches

### Instructions

1. Mix the sliced peaches, raspberries, lime juice, and honey together in a large bowl until the fruit is lightly coated with honey.
2. Add the orange juice and pineapple juice to the fruit mixture in the blender.
3. Blend the mixture until it achieves a smooth consistency.
4. Make the mixture smooth by blending it until there are no more lumps.
5. Transfer the mixture into a deep container with a lid and freeze it for around 5 to 6 hours, or until it is ready to be served.
6. When ready to serve, allow the sorbet to sit at room temperature for about 5 minutes. This will make it much easier to scoop.
7. Scoop the sorbet into bowls or glasses and enjoy!

## 21. RASPBERRY SORBET

Prep Time: 8 minutes

Freeze Time: 1 day

Total Time: 1 day 8 minutes

Serving: 4

### *Ingredients*

- 3 tbsp monk fruit sweetener
- 3 cups of fresh washed raspberries
- Optional: 1 tbsp raw agave nectar

### *Instructions*

1. Mix together the fresh raspberries, monk fruit sweetener, and raw agave nectar (if using) in a bowl of medium size.
2. Use a fork or spatula to mash the raspberries until they release their juice and the sweetener is dissolved.
3. Carefully transfer the raspberry mixture into a pint-sized CREAMi container, ensuring it does not go above the MAX FILL line. Secure the lid onto the container.
4. Put the container in the freezer, ensuring it is leveled, and freeze it for 24 hours.
5. Remove the container from the freezer, take off the lid, and put it in the outer bowl of a Ninja CREAMi.
6. Attach the paddle to the lid and attach the lid to the outer bowl.
7. Plug in the Ninja CREAMi and place the bowl on the base.
8. Press the power button and select LITE ICE CREAM.
9. Once the unit shuts off, remove the bowl from the base and take off the lid.
10. If the sorbet is crumbly, reattach the lid and put the bowl back on the base. Select RE-SPIN. You can repeat this step twice if necessary.
11. When the sorbet reaches the desired consistency, serve immediately.

# NINJA CREAMI GALATO RECIPES

## 22. PUMPKIN PIE GELATO

Prep Time: 20 minutes

Cook Time: 1 day

Freeze Time: 1 day

Total Time: 1 day 20 minutes

Serving: 1 pint

### Ingredients

- 1 Cup of Whole Milk
- 1/2 Cup of Heavy Cream
- 1/3 Cup of Granulated Sugar
- 1/2 Tsp Pumpkin Pie Spice Extract
- 1 Tsp Pumpkin Spice
- 1 Tbsp Light Corn Syrup
- 1/2 Cup of Pumpkin Purée
- 3 Large Egg Yolks
- Optional: 1/4 Tsp Nutmeg

### Instructions

1. In a saucepan, whisk together the egg yolks, corn syrup, and granulated sugar until fully combined.
2. Add the pumpkin puree, heavy cream, whole milk, pumpkin pie spice extract, pumpkin spice, and nutmeg (if using) to the saucepan. Stir the mixture until all ingredients are well combined
3. Place the saucepan on the stove over medium heat. Keep stirring the mixture until it reaches 165 degrees Fahrenheit on an instant-read thermometer.
4. Once the mixture reaches 165 degrees Fahrenheit on an instant-read thermometer, turn off the stove and remove the saucepan from the heat. Next, strain the mixture through a mesh strainer directly into a Ninja Creami pint container.
5. Put the pint container into a bowl filled with ice and cold water until it is cooled.
6. Place the lid onto the pint container and freeze it for a duration of 24 hours.

7. Once 24 hours have passed, remove the pint from the freezer and then take off the lid.
8. Put the pint container into the Ninja Creami's outer bowl.
9. Choose gelato optionand finish the process then take out pint from Ninja Creami, serve and enjoy homemade pumpkin gelato.

## 23. RICOTTA GELATO WITH PISTACHIO AND FIGS

Prep Time: 6 hours

Cook Time: 20 minutes

Total Time: 6 hours 20 minutes

Serving: 1 quart

### *Ingredients*

**For The Fig Swirl**

- Pinch of salt
- Water, as needed
- 10 ounces fresh figs, quartered
- 2 tbsp honey

**For The Pistachio Swirl**

- 1 tbsp sugar
- ½ cups of helled pistachios, lightly toasted
- ¼-½ cup of milk, plus more as needed

**For The Ricotta Ice Cream**

- ¾ cup of sugar
- 1 cup of milk
- 1 cup of heavy cream
- 4 egg yolks
- 2 cups of whole milk ricotta
- Pinch of salt

## *Instructions*

### Make The Fig Swirl

1. To start, preheat the oven to 400 degrees. Then, line a sheet pan with parchment paper and place the quartered figs, honey, and salt on top.
2. Mix the ingredients together with your hands and spread them evenly on the pan. Bake for approximately 20 minutes, until the figs are caramelized and bubbling. While the figs are still hot, mash them into small pieces with a fork.
3. If necessary, use water to loosen the mixture. Once the mixture is mashed, transfer it to a bowl and let it cool. Cover the bowl and refrigerate until it is needed.

### Make The Pistachio Swirl

1. Put the shelled pistachios and sugar in a food processor and pulse on high until the mixture is sandy in texture.
2. Add ¼ cup of milk to the mixture and continue blending until it becomes a smooth paste.
3. Gradually add more milk as needed to achieve a pourable but still thick consistency, similar to pancake batter.
4. Cover the pistachio mixture and store it in the refrigerator until it's needed.

### Make The Ricotta Ice Cream

1. Place a strainer over a bowl and line it with paper towels or cheesecloth.
2. Add the ricotta to the strainer and let it drain for approximately one hour.
3. In a medium saucepan over medium heat, combine milk, sugar, and salt, whisking until the sugar has dissolved.
4. Whisk the egg yolks in a separate bowl to break them up.
5. While continuously whisking, slowly pour the milk mixture over the egg yolks.
6. Pour the mixture back into the saucepan, turn the heat down to low, and use a rubber spatula to stir until it is thick enough to coat the back of a spoon.
7. Strain the mixture through the strainer to remove any lumps, then whisk in the ricotta and heavy cream.
8. Cover and chill for at least 4 hours, with overnight being preferable.
9. Follow the manufacturer's instructions to pour the ice cream mixture into an ice cream maker and process it.
10. Once the ice cream has finished churning, transfer half to a container, then sprinkle half of the fig and pistachio mixtures on top.

11. Use a butter knife to gently swirl in the fig and pistachio. Repeat the process with the remaining ice cream, fig, and pistachio. Quickly transfer the container to the freezer and let it freeze for several hours, preferably overnight. Enjoy!

## 24. MAPLE GELATO

Prep Time: 5 Mins

Freeze Time : 1 Day

Spin Time: 3 Mins

Total Time:  1 Day 8 Mins

Serving:  4

### *Ingredients*

- 1 tbsp maple syrup
- 1 tsp maple extract (optional)
- 4 large egg yolks
- 1 cup of whole milk
- 1/2 cup of + 1 tbsp light brown sugar
- 1/3 cup of heavy cream

### *Instructions*

1. In a small saucepan, whisk egg yolks, maple syrup, sugar, and maple extract until the sugar is completely dissolved.
2. Add heavy cream and milk to the saucepan and stir to combine.
3. Place the saucepan on medium heat and stir constantly with a rubber spatula. Cook until the temperature reaches 165°F–175°F on an instant-read thermometer. Remove the base from heat and strain through a fine-mesh strainer into an empty CREAMi™. Place the pint into an ice bath. Once cooled, cover the pint with the storage lid and freeze for 24 hours.
4. Take the pint from the freezer and remove the lid. Place the pint in the outer bowl of the Ninja Creami. Install the Creamerizer™ Paddle onto the outer bowl lid and lock the lid assembly on the outer bowl. Place the bowl assembly on the motor base and twist the handle right to raise the platform and lock it in place. Choose the GELATO setting.
5. When the processing is complete, add mix-ins or remove the gelato from the pint and serve immediately.

## 25. NINJA CREAMI LEMON GELATO

Prep Time: 15 minutes

Cook Time: 10 minutes

Total Time: 15 minutes

Serving: 4

### Ingredients

- 3 Tbsp Jell-O Lemon Flavor Instant Pudding
- 1 Tbsp Georgia Peach flavored Whiskey
- 1 Tbsp Torani Peach Syrup
- 1 ¾ Cups of Fairlife Whole Milk

### Instructions

1. Add all the ingredients into a Ninja Creami pint and whisk for 2 minutes until well combined.
2. Cover the pint with its lid and place it on a level surface in the freezer for 24 hours to allow it to freeze.
3. After 24 hours, remove the pint from the freezer and place it into the outer bowl of the Ninja Creami machine. Choose the "Gelato" function and let it process the mixture until it reaches a creamy and smooth texture.
4. Scoop the gelato into serving bowls or cones and enjoy the rich and indulgent taste of your homemade frounceen treat!

# 26. NINJA CREAMI GELATO RECIPES (LIMONCELLO GELATO)

Prep Time: 20 Mins

Cooking Time: 30 Mins

Total Time: 50 Mins

Serving: 4

## Ingredients
- 2 cups of Whole Milk
- ¾ Cups of Vanilla Bean Lemon Curd
- ½ cups of Short breadcrumbs
- 4 Egg yolks
- ¼ cups of Limoncello
- 1 cup of Heavy Cream
- Half (1/2) cups of Sugar

## Instructions
1. In a large bowl, beat the egg yolks and sugar together until the mixture is fluffy and smooth.
2. In a large pan, warm the milk and cream over medium heat until small bubbles form around the edges and light steam rises above.
3. Gradually pour the warm milk mixture into the egg blend, whisking constantly.
4. Pour the combined mixture back into the pan and cook over medium heat, stirring constantly until it thickens and coats the spoon (about 170 degrees Fahrenheit).
5. Pour the limoncello into a bowl placed in an ice bath and refrigerate for 4 to 6 hours until completely cooled. Once cooled, cover the bowl.
6. Once the mixture is cooled, mix it right away before hardening. Pour half of it into a sealed receptacle.
7. Dollop in some lemon curd and use a knife to mix it up with the ice cream.
8. Mix in half of the crumbled shortbread biscuits.
9. Repeat step 6, 7, and 8 for the remaining ice cream mixture, lemon curd, and shortbread biscuits.
10. Close the container tightly and put it in the freezer overnight. And Serve

## 27. BLUEBERRY CHEESECAKE GELATO

Prep Time: 5 minutes

Total Time: 1 Day 15 minutes

Serving: 4

### Ingredients

- 1/4 cup of cream cheese
- 3-6 drops of purple food coloring (adjust color to preference)
- 1 tsp vanilla extract
- 1 cup of whole milk
- 2 large graham crackers, broken into 1-inch pieces
- 1/3 cup of heavy cream
- 3 tbsp granulated sugar
- 4 large egg yolks
- 3 tbsp wild blueberry preserves

### Instructions

1. In a small saucepan, mix together the egg yolks, sugar, vanilla extract, and blueberry preserves until fully combined and the sugar is dissolved.
2. Add the heavy cream, milk, and cream cheese to the saucepan and stir to combine.
3. Place the saucepan on the stove over medium heat, constantly stirring with a whisk or rubber spatula. Cook until the temperature reaches 165-175°F on an instant-read thermometer.
4. Remove the base from heat and strain it through a fine-mesh strainer into an empty CREAMi Pint. Add food coloring and adjust the color to your preference. Place the pint into an ice bath. Once cooled, put the storage lid on the pint and freeze for 24 hours.
5. Take the pint out of the freezer, remove the lid from the pint, and use the Quick Start Guide for information on bowl assembly and unit interaction.
6. Select the ICE CREAM function.
7. Use a spoon to create a 1.5-inch wide hole that reaches the bottom of the pint. Add 2 graham crackers that have been broken into 1-inch pieces to the hole and process again using the MIX-IN program. Serve immediately.

## 28. CHOCOLATE CHERRY STRACCIATELLA GELATO

Prep Time: 45 minutes

Cook Time: 15 minutes

Freeze Time: 8 hours

Total Time: 8 hours 10 minutes

Serving: 8

## *Ingredients*

- One vanilla bean or 1 tsp vanilla extract
- 4 ounces bittersweet chocolate, coarsely chopped
- 3/4 cup of sugar
- Fresh cherries for serving
- 6 tbsp cherry preserves
- 4 large egg yolks at room temperature
- 1 cup of heavy cream
- 2 cups of 2% milk

## *Instructions*

1. In a deep saucepan, combine milk, heavy cream, and 1/2 cup of sugar. Split open the vanilla bean and scrape the seeds into the pan. Heat over medium heat until bubbles start to form, but do not let them boil. Remove from heat and let it steep for 15 minutes.
2. In a bowl, whisk egg yolks and the remaining sugar. Slowly add 1/2 cup of the warm milk mixture to the yolks, whisking constantly. Add another 1/2 cup of the warm mixture and whisk to combine.
3. Pour the egg yolk mixture back into the pan with the remaining milk mixture. Remove the vanilla bean and heat over medium heat, constantly stirring with a spatula, until the mixture thickens and coats the back of the spatula for about 10 minutes.
4. Remove from heat and strain through a fine mesh sieve. Let cool at room temperature for 15 minutes, then cover and refrigerate for at least 2 hours or overnight.
5. For 15-20 minutes, churn the mixture in an ice cream maker according to the manufacturer's instructions.
6. While the gelato is churning, melt the bittersweet chocolate over a double boiler. Place in a zip lock bag, close, and cut the tip.
7. With the ice cream maker still churning the gelato, slowly drizzle the melted chocolate inside.
8. Transfer the gelato to a container and swirl in the cherry preserves. Freeze overnight.
9. Serve with fresh cherries.

## 29. EGGNOG ICE CREAM GELATO

Prep Time: 5 minutes

Cook Time: 2 minutes

Freeze Time: 1 day

Total Time: 1 day 7 minutes

Serving: 1 pint

### Ingredients

- 2 cups of eggnog
- Optional: 1/8 tsp ground cinnamon, 1/8 tsp ground nutmeg

### Instructions

1. Take a Ninja Creami pint and pour in 2 cups of eggnog, being careful not to fill it above the maximum line.
2. If you want to add some extra flavor, sprinkle 1/8 tsp ground cinnamon and 1/8 tsp ground nutmeg into the eggnog and stir it in.
3. Put the lid on the pint and move it to a flat surface in your freezer.
4. Let the mixture freeze for a whole day, about 24 hours.
5. Once the time has passed, take out the pint from the freezer and remove the lid.
6. Insert the pint into the outer bowl apparatus and secure it into the Ninja Creami machine.
7. Press the Gelato button to begin the cycle and let it run for approximately 2 minutes.
8. After the cycle is finished, take out the pint from the apparatus.
9. If the ice cream seems to be crumbly or grainy, put the pint back into the Ninja Creami machine and press the Re-spin button to run the cycle again. This should help to smooth out the texture.
10. Serve the eggnog ice cream as desired, either on its own or as a delicious accompaniment to Christmas cookies or pie. Enjoy!

## 30. PEACHES AND CREAM OATMEAL GELATO

Prep Time: 1 Hrs

Freeze Time: 1 Day

Total Time: 1 Day 1 Hrs

Serving: 1

## *Ingredients*

- 2 Tbsp Yogurt
- 2 Individual Packages Instant Oatmeal Peaches and Cream
- 1 Cup of Water (Hot)
- 1 Tbsp Buttery Cinnamon Roll Seasoning (Flavor God )
- 1 Tbsp Heavy Cream Powder (Hoosier Hill Farm )

## *Instructions*

1. In a small mixing bowl, pour in the Peaches and Cream instant oatmeal and cover it with hot water. Allow it to cool.
2. Once the oatmeal has cooled, transfer it to a pint container for the Ninja Creami.
3. Add in the heavy cream powder, cinnamon roll seasoning, and yogurt. Mix thoroughly either with a spoon or by using the milkshake process on the Ninja Creami.
4. Freeze the mixture on a level surface for 24 hours.
5. After 24 hours, take the container out of the freezer and place it in the outer bowl.
6. Add the mixture to the Ninja Creami and process it using the Gelato function.
7. If a softer gelato is preferred, re-spin the mixture once.

## 31. NINJA CREAMI PEPPERMINT STICK GELATO

Prep Time: 5 Mins

Freeze Time: 1 Day

Total Time: 1 Day 5 mins

Serving: 1

### INGREDIENTS

- 3/4 cups of Heavy Cream
- 1 tsp Peppermint Extract
- 2 Egg Yolks
- 1/2 tsp Vanilla Extract
- 1/4 cup of Crushed Candy Cane (Plus More for Optional Mix-In)
- 1/3 cup of Granulated Sugar
- 1 cup of Whole Milk

### INSTRUCTION

1. To make this delicious peppermint stick gelato recipe, start by crushing a few candy canes until you have 1/4 cup of crushed candy canes. You can use a mallet or your hands to do this. Note that you can also use peppermints or a peppermint stick as a substitute.
2. In a pot, combine 1 tsp of peppermint extract, 1/2 tsp of vanilla extract, 1/3 cup of granulated sugar, 1 cup of whole milk, 3/4 cup of heavy cream, 2 egg yolks, and 1/4 cup of crushed candy canes. Cook this mixture on medium heat for 5 minutes, constantly whisking to ensure that the eggs don't scramble.
3. Pour the mixture into a Ninja Creami container, making sure not to go over the max fill line. Wait for the pint to cool, and then place it into the freezer on a flat surface. Freeze for 24 hours.

4. Then, remove the pint from the freezer and plug in your Ninja Creami machine. Take off the lid from the pint container.
5. Put the pint container securely into the outer bowl of the Creami machine. Cover it with the lid and twist it to the right until it locks into place. Press the "Gelato" button and wait for the machine to work its magic.
6. Once the process is complete, hold the button on the left side of the Creami to twist the bowl to the left and remove it from the machine. Twist the lid off of the outer bowl and remove the pint.
7. You can optionally carve a hole down the center of the spun gelato and add additional crushed candy cane (about 1/4 cup ofor as much as you prefer).
8. If you like, place the pint back into the Ninja Creami and select the "Mix-In" button. When the machine is finished, remove the pint from the cream.

## 32. BROWNIE BATTER GELATO

Prep Time: 5 minutes

Cook Time: 10 minutes

Rest Time: 24 hours

Total Time: 24 hours 15 minutes

Serving: 1 pint

### Ingredients

- 2 egg yolks
- 3/4 cup of heavy cream
- 1/4 cup of brownie mix
- A dash of salt
- 1 cup of whole milk
- 1/3 cup of granulated sugar
- 1 tsp of vanilla extract

### Instructions

1. In a pot, combine 1 tsp vanilla extract, 1/3 cup ofgranulated sugar, 1 cup ofwhole milk, 3/4 cup of heavy cream, 2 egg yolks, 1/4 cup of brownie mix, and a dash of salt.
2. Place the pot on the stove at medium heat and whisk the mixture constantly for 5 minutes to avoid scrambled eggs.
3. Pour the mixture into a Ninja Creami pint container, making sure not to exceed the max fill line.
4. Allow the pint to cool down, and place it on a flat surface in the freezer. Let it freeze for 24 hours.After 24 hours, remove the pint from the freezer and plug in your Ninja Creami machine.
5. Take off the lid from the pint and get the Ninja Creami outer bowl.
6. Securely place the pint into the outer bowl and cover it with the lid. Twist the outer bowl into the machine to the right until it locks into place.
7. Press the "Gelato" button and patiently wait for the machine to work its magic.
8. Once the process is complete, hold the button on the left side of the Creami to twist the bowl to the left and remove it from the machine.
9. Twist the lid off the outer bowl and take the pint out.
10. Voila! Your brownie batter gelato is now ready to be savored and enjoyed.

## 33. BUTTER PECAN GELATO

Prep Time: 15 minutes

Cook Time: 1 day

Total Time: 1 day 15 minutes

Serving: 1 pint

### *Ingredients*

- 1 tsp of butter flavor extract
- 1/3 cup of whole milk
- 1 tbsp of light corn syrup
- 1 cup of heavy cream
- 4 large egg yolks
- 5 tbsp of granulated sugar
- 1/3 cup of pecan pieces

### *Instructions*

1. In a saucepan, whisk together the egg yolks, corn syrup, and sugar until fully combined.
2. Pour in the heavy cream, whole milk, and butter extract, and continue to stir until well combined.
3. Place the saucepan on medium heat and continue stirring until the mixture reaches 165 degrees Fahrenheit on an instant-read thermometer.
4. Turn off the heat and pour the mixture through a mesh strainer directly into a Ninja Creami pint container.
5. Place the pint container into a bowl of ice and ice water until it cools down.
6. Once cooled, put the lid on the pint container and freeze it for 24 hours.
7. After 24 hours, take the pint container out of the freezer and remove the lid.
8. Place the pint container into the outer bowl of the Ninja Creami machine.

9. Choose the gelato process and wait for the machine to finish.
10. Once the process is complete, remove the pint container from the Ninja Creami and use a spoon to create a small tunnel through the middle of the gelato.
11. Add the pecan pieces into the tunnel and mix them into the gelato.
12. Put the pint container back into the outer bowl of the Ninja Creami machine and select the mix-ins process.
13. When the process is complete, remove the pint container from the machine and serve your delicious pecan batter gelato.

## 34. BLACK CHERRY GELATO

Prep Time: 40 minutes

Cook Time: 1 day

Total Time: 1 day 40 minutes

Serving: 1 pint

### Ingredients

- 5 tbsp of granulated sugar
- 1 tbsp of light corn syrup
- 1 cup of heavy cream
- 1 tsp of almond extract
- 1/3 cup of whole milk
- 1 cup of frounceen and quartered black cherries
- 4 large egg yolks

### Instructions

1. In a saucepan, combine the egg yolks, corn syrup, and sugar. Use a whisk to fully combine the ingredients.
2. Pour in the heavy cream, milk, and almond extract. Continue to stir until well combined.
3. Cook the mixture over medium heat on the stove. Continue to stir until the mixture reaches 165 degrees Fahrenheit on an instant-read thermometer.
4. Turn off the stove, remove from heat, and pour the mixture through a mesh strainer directly into a Ninja Creami pint container.
5. Place the pint container into a bowl of ice and ice water until cooled.
6. Put the lid on the pint container and freeze it for 24 hours.
7. After 24 hours, take the pint out of the freezer and remove the lid.
8. Place the pint into the outer bowl of the Ninja Creami machine.
9. Choose the gelato process and let the machine work its magic.
10. When the process is complete, remove the pint from the Ninja Creami.
11. Manually fold in the quartered black cherries and serve. Enjoy your homemade gelato!

## 35. EGGNOG GELATO

Prep Time: 1 minute

Freeze Time: 1 day

Total Time: 1 day 1 minute

Serving: 1 pint

### *Ingredients*

- 16 ounces of eggnog
- Optional: nutmeg, cinnamon, vanilla extract or paste, bourbon or brandy

### *Instructions*

1. Firstly, pour the eggnog into an empty pint container and seal it with the lid. Allow it to freeze for 24 hours.
2. After the elapsed time, remove the pint container from the freezer and take off the lid.
3. Next, place the pint container into the outer bowl of the Ninja Creami machine and lock it into place by turning it.
4. Press the GELATO button and allow the machine to perform its function. During this process, the eggnog will mix together and become extremely creamy.
5. Once the gelato function is complete, turn the outer bowl and remove it from the Ninja Creami machine. If the eggnog has a dry or crumbly texture, dig a hole in the center and add a tbsp or two of eggnog or milk, then re-spin.
6. Your homemade eggnog gelato is now ready to be served! You can optionally sprinkle some nutmeg or cinnamon or add a splash of bourbon or brandy on top to enhance the flavor. Enjoy this delicious treat to the fullest!

# NINJA CREAMI ICE CREAM MIX - INS

## 36. S'MORES ICE CREAM

Prep Time: 7 minutes

Cook Time: 8 minutes

Freeze Time: 1 day

Total Time: 1 day 15 minutes

Serving: 2

## *Ingredients*

**Ice Cream Base**

- 3/4 cup of heavy cream
- 1 tbsp softened cream cheese
- 1/2 cup of whole milk
- 1/3 cup of granulated sugar
- Eight large marshmallows
- One tsp of sea salt

**Mix-Ins**

- 1/2 cup of graham cracker, broken, for mix-in
- 1/4 cup of mini dark chocolate chips for mix-in
- 

**Topping**

- Pinch of sea salt

## Instructions

1. Preheat the broiler and line a baking sheet with aluminum foil. Arrange the marshmallows on the baking sheet and broil them for 5 to 7 minutes or until they are browned. Once done, set them aside to cool.
2. Take a large microwave-safe bowl and microwave the cream cheese for 20 seconds. Add the sugar and sea salt to the bowl and whisk or mix with a rubber spatula until the mixture becomes smooth and creamy, like frosting.
3. Slowly pour in the milk and heavy cream while continuing to stir the mixture until the sugar is fully dissolved and the ingredients are fully combined.
4. Add the cooled marshmallows to the mixture and stir to combine. Pour the mixture into an empty CREAMi™ pint and cover it with a storage lid. Freeze the mixture for 24 hours.
5. Once frounceen, remove the pint from the freezer and remove the lid. Place the pint in the outer bowl and attach the CREAMi Paddle to the outer bowl lid. Lock the lid assembly onto the outer bowl and place the bowl assembly on the motor base. Twist the handle to raise the platform and lock it in place.
6. Select the ICE CREAM function.
7. Using a spoon, create a 1 ½-inch wide hole in the ice cream that reaches the bottom of the pint. Add the graham cracker crumbs and mini dark chocolate chips into the hole and process again using the MIX-IN program.
8. Once processing is complete, remove the ice cream from the pint and top it with a pinch of sea salt. Serve immediately, and enjoy your homemade marshmallow ice cream with graham crackers and dark chocolate chips!

## 37. RASPBERRY WHITE TRUFFLE ICE CREAM

Prep Time: 5 minutes

Freeze Time: 1 day

Total Time: 1 day 5 minutes

Serving: 1 pint

### *Ingredients*

- 3/4 cup of heavy whipping cream
- 1 cup of milk
- 1 tbsp raspberry preserves
- 1 tbsp cream cheese, at room temperature
- 1/4 cup of raspberries, cut in half
- 1/3 cup of sugar

**Mix-Ins**

- 3 white chocolate truffles, cut in quarters
- 1/4 cup ofraspberries, cut in half

**Instructions**

1. In a mixing bowl, combine the cream cheese, sugar, and raspberry preserves. Whisk together until the sugar starts to dissolve and all ingredients are fully combined.
2. Whisk the heavy whipping cream and milk into the bowl containing the cream cheese, sugar, and raspberry preserves mixture. It may take a minute or two to fully combine the ingredients due to the thick consistency of the raspberry preserves mixture.
3. Incorporate approximately 6-8 raspberries, cut in half, to the mixture.
4. Place the ice cream base into an empty Ninja Creami pint container and freeze it for 24 hours.
5. Once the 24 hours have passed, take the pint container out of the freezer and remove the lid.
6. Lock the outer bowl of the Ninja Creami machine into place by putting the pint inside it.
7. Press the ICE CREAM button to initiate the ice cream function, allowing the mixture to blend and attain a creamy texture.

8. After the ice cream function has completed, use a spoon to create a hole through the center of the ice cream by turning the outer bowl. This is where you will add your mix-ins.
9. Cut the raspberries in half and quarter the white chocolate truffles, then add them into the hole created in the ice cream, which should be about 1/4 cup of raspberries and 3 white chocolate truffles.
10. Put the outer bowl with the pint back into the Ninja Creami machine and lock it into place, then select the MIX-IN function.
11. After the MIX-IN cycle is completed by the Ninja Creami, take out the outer bowl from the machine.
12. You can now savor your delicious ice cream!

## 38. FROUNCEEN HOT CHOCOLATE ICE CREAM

Prep Time: 5 minutes

Freeze Time: 1 day

Total Time: 1 day 5 minutes

Serving: 1 pint

### *Ingredients*

- 1/4 cup of half and half
- 1 individual serving packet (0.73 ounces) of Swiss Miss hot cocoa mix
- 1/4 cup of Silk Sweet and Creamy almond milk creamer
- 1 cup of whole chocolate milk

### *Instructions*

1. In a medium-sized bowl, combine the chocolate milk, half and half, and almond milk creamer.
2. Microwave the bowl on high power until the milk is hot but not boiling, which takes around 2 minutes.
3. Remove the bowl from the microwave and immediately add the hot cocoa mix packet to the mixture.
4. Whisk the mixture well until fully combined. The hot milk will help the cocoa mix to combine.
5. Pour the fully combined mixture into a pint container and cool it in the refrigerator for 10 minutes.
6. Give the mixture one more quick whisk, and then place the container in the freezer for 24 hours.
7. Put the pint container into the Ninja Creami machine and process it on the Ice Cream set.
8. Once the process has been completed, remove the pint from the Ninja Creami machine.
9. If desired, serve the ice cream with a sprinkling of mini marshmallows.
10. Enjoy your homemade chocolate ice cream!

## 39. BANANA CHOCOLATE CHIP LITE ICE CREAM

Prep Time: 5 minutes

Freeze Time: 12 hours

Total Time: 12 hours 5 minutes

Serving: 1 pint

### *Ingredients*

- 1/2 cup of Almond Milk
- 3 ripe bananas, mashed
- 1/4 cup of chocolate chips

### *Instructions*

1. Mash the bananas in the Creami Pint.
2. Pour in the Toasted Coconut Almond Milk up to the max fill line.
3. Freeze the mixture for at least 12 hours.
4. Place the Ninja Creami pint into the outer bowl and insert it into the machine.
5. A process on Lite Ice Cream and respin twice.
6. If adding chocolate chips, create a 1.5-inch wide hole at the bottom of the pint and add the chips. A process on Mix In.
7. Enjoy your homemade ice cream!

## 40. COPYCAT CHUNKY MONKEY ICE CREAM

Prep Time: 10 minutes

Freeze Time: 1 day

Total Time: 1 day 10 minutes

Serving: 1 pint

### Ingredients

- 1/2 cup of whole milk
- 2 TBSP chopped walnuts
- 1 tsp vanilla extract
- 2 small ripe bananas, mashed
- 1/2 cup of heavy whipping cream
- 1/4 cup of chopped chocolate chunks
- 1 TBSP maple syrup (optional)

### Instructions

1. Combine the mashed bananas, whole milk, heavy cream, and vanilla extract in a small bowl or a Ninja Creami pint.
2. Blend the mixture using an immersion blender or a regular blender until there are no chunks of banana left.
3. Taste the mixture and add maple syrup if you want it sweeter.
4. Close the lid on the pint and put it in the freezer for 24 hours.
5. Once the mixture is frounceen, remove the pint from the freezer and take off the lid. Insert the pint into the Ninja Creami bowl and lock the lid.
6. Select the Ice Cream function and let it run for about 2 minutes.
7. Using a spoon, create a well in the center of the ice cream that goes all the way to the bottom of the pint.
8. Mix together the chocolate chunks and walnuts, and then add the mixture to the well.
9. Put the bowl back into the machine and use the Mix In function to incorporate the nuts and chocolate into the ice cream.
10. Enjoy your homemade ice cream made with creamy milk, ripe bananas, and delicious chunks of chocolate and walnuts!

## 41. CHOCOLATE PEANUT BUTTER BANANA ICE CREAM

Prep Time: 5 Mins

Freeze Time: 1 Day

Total Time: 1 Day 5 mins

Serving: 1

### *Ingredients*

- ¼ Cup of Chocolate Chunks (or Chips)
- ½ Cup of Peanut Butter
- ¼ Cup of Half and Half

**Mix-Ins**

- 4-5 Bananas (More or less depending on the size of the bananas- Ripe- cut into 1-2 inch chunks. I used small bananas- if using very large bananas, you may only need 2 or 3. )
- ¼ Cup of Cocoa Powder (Dark Cocoa Powder)

### *Instructions*

1. Combine 2 ripe bananas, 1/4 cup of peanut butter, 1/4 cup of cocoa powder, and 1/2 cup of half and half in a blender.
2. Blend the mixture until smooth and well combined.
3. Pour the mixture into a Ninja Creami Pint container.
4. Put the lid on the pint container and freeze on a level surface for 24 hours.
5. After 24 hours, remove the pint from the freezer and remove the lid.
6. Place the Ninja Creami pint into the outer bowl.
7. Place the outer bowl with the pint in it into the Ninja Creami machine and turn until the outer bowl locks into place.
8. Push the ICE CREAM button. During the ice cream function, the ice cream will mix together and become very creamy. And Re-spin once.
9. Once the ice cream function has ended, turn the outer bowl and release it from the Ninja Creami machine.
10. Use a spoon to dig a hole down the center of the ice cream. Pour in 1/2 cup of chocolate chunks and put the pint back into the Ninja Creami machine.
11. Choose the "Mix-Ins" function and process. Once it has finished processing, remove it from the machine.
12. Your chocolate peanut butter banana ice cream is ready to eat! Enjoy!

## 42. MINT CHOCOLATE ICE CREAM

Prep Time: 5 Minutes

Freeze Time: 1 Day

Total Time: 1 Day 5 Minutes

Serving: 1 Pint

### Ingredients

4 Drops (4 Drops) of Green Food Coloring

2 Tbsp (2 Tbsp) Instant Pudding Mix (Vanilla)

⅓ Cup of (66 ⅔ g) Sugar

1 Cup of (244 g) Milk

½ Cup of (121 g) Half and Half

½ Tsp (½ Tsp) Peppermint Extract

### Ingredients

1. Combine all ice cream base ingredients in the Ninja Creami pint container.
2. Mix the ingredients well with a whisk or immersion blender.
3. Put the lid on the pint and freeze it on a level surface for 24 hours.
4. After 24 hours, remove the pint from the freezer and take off the lid.
5. Place the Ninja Creami pint into the outer bowl.
6. Place the outer bowl with the pint in it into the Ninja Creami machine and turn it until the outer bowl locks into place.
7. Push the ICE CREAM button.
8. During the ice cream function, the ice cream will mix together and become very creamy.
9. Once the ice cream function has ended, turn the outer bowl and release it from the Ninja Creami machine. Dig a hole in the center of the ice cream and squirt in the magic shell.
10. Drizzle the magic shell over the top of the ice cream as well.
11. Let it sit for about a minute so that the magic shell sets up and gets hard.
12. Put the pint back into the Ninja Creami and process it on the "Mix-Ins" function.
13. Once the Ninja Creami is finished processing, remove it from the machine.
14. Your ice cream is ready to eat! Enjoy!

## 43. NINJA CREAMI PINA COLADA LIGHT ICE CREAM

Prep Time: 1 Min

Freeze Time: 1 Day

Total Time: 1 Day 1 Min

Serving: 1

### *Ingredients*

**Ice Cream Base**

- ½ Cup of Pineapple (Canned tidbits- small pieces)
- 1 ¼ Cups of Coconut Cream (Canned-Unsweetened)

**Mix-Ins**

- 1 Tbsp Pineapple (Chopped)
- 1 Tbsp Toasted Coconut

### *Ingredients*

1. Start by pouring coconut cream and pineapple into an empty Ninja Creami pint container. Make sure not to stir the mixture before freezing it. Place the container in the freezer and let it freeze for 24 hours.
2. After 24 hours, remove the pint container from the freezer and take off the lid.
3. Put the Ninja Creami pint container into the outer bowl, then place the outer bowl into the Ninja Creami machine. Turn the bowl until it locks into place. Select the Lite Ice Cream button and let the machine work its magic. The ice cream will mix together and become extra creamy during this step.
4. Once the Lite Ice Cream function is complete, take out the outer bowl and use a spoon to make a hole in the center of the ice cream that goes from top to bottom. This is where you will add your mix-ins. Add 1 tbsp of toasted coconut and 1 tbsp of chopped pineapple to the hole.
5. Place the outer bowl with the pint back into the Ninja Creami machine and lock it into place. Select the MIX-IN function to mix the ingredients together.
6. When the MIX-IN cycle is complete, remove the outer bowl from the machine.
7. Your pineapple and coconut ice cream is now ready to eat! Enjoy its creamy texture and tropical flavors.

## 44. BANANA PUDDING ICE CREAM

Prep Time: 15 minutes

Freeze Time: 1 day

Total Time: 1 day 15 minutes

Serving: 1 pint

### Ingredients

- 3/4 cup of heavy cream
- 1 dash of ground nutmeg
- 1 cup of whole milk
- 2 bananas, fresh
- 1 tsp vanilla extract or paste
- 4 Nilla Wafers
- 1.7 ounces banana cream instant pudding (1/2 of a 3.4-ounce box)
- 1 tbsp cream cheese at room temperature
- 1 dash of ground cinnamon

### Instructions

1. In a blender, mix the cream cheese, vanilla extract, heavy cream, milk, 1 banana, and instant pudding until smooth.
2. Mash the other banana and add it to the Ninja Creami pint.
3. Pour the liquid mixture into the pint container and add a sprinkle of cinnamon and nutmeg.
4. Cover the pint and freeze it for 24 hours.
5. Remove the pint from the freezer and place it in the outer bowl.
6. Select the "Ice cream" button and let the unit process.
7. When finished, remove the pint and create a tunnel down the center of the ice cream. Add 2 Nilla Wafers.
8. Select the "Mix-ins" button and process.
9. Serve with 1 Nilla Wafer and crumbled Nilla Wafer on top. Enjoy your delicious treat

## 45. BLUEBERRY PIE ICE CREAM

Prep Time: 5 minutes

Cook Time: 10 minutes

Freeze Time: 1 day

Total Time: 1 day 15 minutes

Serving: 1 pint

### *Ingredients*

- Ice Cream Base:
- 2 tbsp vanilla-flavored instant pudding mix
- 1 cup of milk
- ½ cup of half and half

**Pie Filling:**

- 1 cup of fresh blueberries
- ½ tsp lemon juice
- ¼ cup of sugar

**Crust:**

- ¼ tsp ground cinnamon
- 1 graham cracker (crushed)
- 1 tsp sugar
- 1 tsp melted butter

## Instructions

1. To make In a small saucepan over medium heat, stir together blueberries, sugar, and lemon juice until the sugar has dissolved and the blueberries have burst about 5 minutes. Set aside to cool.
2. In the Ninja Creami pint container, whisk together milk, half and half, and instant pudding mix.
3. Add the cooled blueberry pie filling mixture to the pint container and mix with the ice cream base.
4. Cover the pint container with the lid and freeze on a level surface for 24 hours.
5. After 24 hours, remove the pint container from the freezer and the lid from the pint.
6. Place the pint container into the outer bowl of the Ninja Creami machine and lock it into place.
7. Press the ICE CREAM button on the machine to mix the ice cream until it becomes creamy.
8. In a separate bowl, combine the crust ingredients and stir until well combined.
9. Once the ice cream function has ended, remove the outer bowl from the machine and dig a hole in the center of the ice cream.
10. Add the crust mixture to the hole.
11. Put the pint container back into the Ninja Creami machine and process on mix-ins.
12. Your ice cream is ready to eat! Enjoy!

## 46. BOOUNCEY CHERRY GARCIA ICE CREAM

Prep Time: 20 minutes

Cook Time: 1 day

Total Time: 1 day 20 minutes

Serving: 1 pint

### Ingredients

- 1 ½ cups of whole milk
- 2-3 tbsp mini semi-sweet chocolate chips
- ⅓ cup of vanilla instant pudding mix (½ small package)
- ½ cup of frounceen dark sweet cherries (cut in half)
- ½ cup of lactose-free half and half
- 2 tbsp cherry whiskey (1 ounce-Bird Dog Whiskey-Black Cherry flavor)

### Instructions

1. In a bowl, whisk together vanilla instant pudding mix, whole milk, lactose-free half and half, and cherry whiskey until fully combined and the mixture has thickened a bit.
2. Pour the mixture into the Ninja Creami pint container and freeze on a level surface for at least 24 hours.
3. Put the pint container into the Ninja Creami machine and process on the Ice Cream set.
4. Remove the pint container from the machine and clear a hole in the bottom of the ice cream in the container.
5. Add the frounceen cherries to the hole and put the pint container back into the Creami machine.
6. Process using the mix-ins function.
7. Remove the pint container from the machine and clear a hole in the bottom of the ice cream in the container.
8. Add the mini semi-sweet chocolate chips to the hole and put the pint container back into the Creami machine.
9. Process using the mix-ins function.
10. Your ice cream is ready to eat! Enjoy!

## 47. BUTTER PECAN ICE CREAM

Prep Time: 5 minutes

Freeze Time: 1 day

Total Time: 1 day 5 minutes

Serving: 1 pint

### *Ingredients*

**Ice Cream Base**

- 1/2 cup of (100 g) sugar
- 1/4 tsp (1/4 tsp) butter flavor (Lorann Oils)
- 1 tbsp (1 tbsp) cream cheese
- 1/4 tsp (1/4 tsp) pecan flavor (Lorann Oils)
- 2/3 cup of (161 1/3 g) half and half
- 1 cup of (244 g) whole milk

**Mix-Ins**

- 2-3 tbsp (2 tbsp) chopped pecans

### *Instructions*

1. Combine all ice cream base ingredients in the Ninja Creami pint container and stir well with a spoon, whisk, or blender until the cream cheese has fully mixed in with the other ingredients.
2. Freeze the pint container on a level surface for 24 hours.
3. After 24 hours, remove the pint from the freezer and take off the lid.
4. Place the Ninja Creami pint into the outer bowl and twist until it locks into place. Put the outer bowl with the pint in it into the Ninja Creami machine and push the ICE CREAM button. During the ice cream function, the ingredients will mix together and become very creamy.
5. Once the ice cream function has ended, turn the outer bowl and release it from the Ninja Creami machine.
6. Use a spoon to create a hole down the center of the ice cream and pour in the chopped pecans.
7. Put the outer bowl lid back on and insert it back into the Ninja Creami machine.
8. Choose the mix-ins function and process.
9. Once the mix-ins function has ended, turn the outer bowl and release it from the Ninja Creami machine.  andwith pecan mix-ins is now ready to eat. Enjoy!

## 48. CHOCOLATE CHIP ICE CREAM

Prep Time: 5 minutes

Freeze Time: 1 day

Total Time: 1 day 5 minutes

Serving: 1 pint

### Ingredients

**Ice Cream Base**

- 1 tbsp room temperature cream cheese
- 1 cup ofwhole milk and 1/3 cup of sugar
- 2/3 cup of half and half

**Mix-Ins**

- 1/3 cup of mini chocolate chips

### Instructions

1. Combine all ingredients for the ice cream base, except for the mini chocolate chips, in the Ninja Creami pint container. Mix well.
2. Freeze the mixture on a level surface for 24 hours.
3. After 24 hours, remove the pint container from the freezer and remove the lid.
4. Place the Ninja Creami pint into the outer bowl and lock it in place by turning the outer bowl.
5. Push the ICE CREAM button on the Ninja Creami machine to start the ice cream function. During this process, the ice cream mixture will become creamy.
6. Once the ice cream function has ended, turn the outer bowl to release it from the machine.
7. Dig a hole in the center of the ice cream and pour in the mini chocolate chips.
8. Put the pint back into the Ninja Creami machine and process it on the "Mix-Ins" function. Repeat this process a second time to ensure that the chocolate chips are distributed evenly throughout the ice cream.
9. Once the Ninja Creami has finished processing, remove the pint container from the machine.
10. Your ice cream is now ready to eat. Enjoy!

## 49. CHOCOLATE PEANUT BUTTER BANANA ICE CREAM

Prep Time: 5 minutes

Additional Time: 1 day

Total Time: 1 day 5 minutes

Serving: 1 pint

### *Ingredients*

- 1/4 cup of half and half
- 1/4 cup of dark cocoa powder
- 1/2 cup of peanut butter
- 4-5 ripe bananas, cut into 1-2 inch

**Mix-Ins**

- 1/4 cup of chocolate chunks or chips

### *Instructions*

1. Combine the bananas, peanut butter, cocoa powder, and half and half in a blender and blend until smooth.
2. Pour the mixture into a pint-sized container that is compatible with the Ninja Creami.
3. Put the lid on the container and freeze it on a level surface for 24 hours.
4. After 24 hours, remove the container from the freezer and remove the lid.
5. Place the Ninja Creami pint into the outer bowl and lock it into place.
6. Select the Ice Cream function and let it run until the ice cream is very creamy.
7. Once the function has ended, turn the outer bowl and release it from the Ninja Creami machine.
8. Use a spoon to create a hole down the center of the ice cream and pour in the chocolate chunks.
9. Put the container back into the Ninja Creami machine and select the Mix-Ins function.
10. Once the mix-ins have been processed, remove the container from the machine and serve your delicious homemade ice cream!

## 50. COOKIES AND CREAM ICE CREAM

Prep Time: 5 minutes

Freeze Time: 1 day

Total Time: 1 day 5 minutes

Serving: 1 pint

### *Ingredients*

**Ice Cream Base**

- 2 tbsp instant vanilla pudding mix
- 1 tsp vanilla extract
- 1 cup of milk
- 1/2 cup of half and half
- 1/3 cup of sugar

**Mix-Ins**

- 4-5 Oreos, smashed or crumbled

### *Instructions*

1. In the Ninja Creami pint container, combine all ingredients except for the Oreos. Mix well.
2. Freeze the mixture on a level surface for 24 hours.
3. After 24 hours, remove the pint from the freezer and take off the lid.
4. Place the Ninja Creami pint into the outer bowl and lock it into place.
5. Press the ICE CREAM button to start the ice cream function. The machine will mix the ice cream together until it becomes creamy.
6. Once the ice cream function is complete, remove the outer bowl from the Ninja Creami machine.
7. Dig a hole in the center of the ice cream and add the crumbled Oreos.
8. Put the pint back into the Ninja Creami and select the "Mix-Ins" function. Repeat this function two more times to thoroughly mix in the Oreos.
9. Once the Ninja Creami is finished processing, remove the pint from the machine.
10. Serve and enjoy your delicious homemade Oreo ice cream!

# NINJA CREMI ICE CREAM

## 51. PEANUT BUTTER ICE CREAM

Prep Time: 1 minutes

Cook Time: 1 minutes

Total Time: 2 minutes

Serving: 8

### *Ingredients*

- 1 13.5 ounce can coconut milk chilled
- 3/4 cup of peanut butter can sub for any nut or seed butter of choice
- 1/4 cup of maple syrup

### *Instructions*

1. To prepare, place a container or loaf pan that can be stored in the freezer inside the freezer compartment.
2. Using a high-speed blender or food processor, blend all of the ingredients until they form a thick and creamy mixture. Be sure to scrape down the sides of the blender or processor regularly to ensure that everything is thoroughly combined.
3. Once the mixture is ready, pour it into the previously chilled container and place it in the freezer. Every 15 minutes during the first hour, remove it from the freezer and stir the mixture before returning it to the freezer to ensure even freezing.
4. Let the ice cream freeze for at least three hours or until completely frounceen.
5. Before serving, allow the ice cream to thaw for 5-10 minutes at room temperature.

## 52. ITALIAN CREMA ICE CREAM

Prep Time: 5 Mins

Cook Time: 1 Day

Total Time: 1 day 5 Mins

Serving: 1

### *Ingredients*

- 16 Ounces Lemonade

**Optional:**

- Sugar or your preferred sweetener to taste.

### *Instructions*

1. In order to make Italian ice, pour 16 ounces of lemonade into a pint container for the Ninja Creami. If desired, add any additional sugar or dairy ingredients. Freeze the pint on a level surface in a cold freezer for a full 24 hours.
2. After 24 hours, take the pint out of the freezer and remove the lid. Place the pint into the outer bowl of the Ninja Creami machine, and turn the bowl until it locks into place. Press the SORBET button to begin the mixing process, which will result in a creamy consistency. This process typically takes around 2 minutes.
3. When the SORBET function is finished, turn the outer bowl to release it from the machine. Next, place the outer bowl with the pint back into the Ninja Creami machine and lock it into place. Select the RE-SPIN function to further enhance the texture of the Italian ice. Remember that you must first remove the pint from the machine before re-spinning it.
4. Once the RE-SPIN cycle is complete, remove the outer bowl from the Ninja Creami machine. Your Italian ice is now ready to be enjoyed!

## 53. KETO PEANUT BUTTER CUP OFICE CREAM

Prep Time: 10 minutes

Cook Time: 1 Day

Total Time: 1 Day 10 minutes

Serving: 2

### Ingredients

- ⅛ tsp salt
- ½ scoop Quest Peanut Butter Protein Powder (½ scoop is 15 grams)
- 3 tbsp Swerve Confectioners
- 2 Quest Peanut Butter Cups of (OPTIONAL: as a replacement for milk chocolate chips)
- ½ ounce Lily's Milk Chocolate Style Baking Chips
- 1 tbsp PBFit Pure Peanut
- 1 cup ofunsweetned vanilla almond milk
- ¼ scant tsp guar gum

### Instructions

1. Blend the ingredients: In a blender or food processor, mix all the ingredients together until a smooth and fully mixed consistency is achieved.
2. Freeze the mixture: Transfer the blended mixture into a Ninja Creami pint container and put it in the freezer. Allow it to freeze for at least 24 hours.
3. Use the Ninja Creami: Once the mixture is frounceen, remove the lid of the pint container and place it in the outer bowl of the Ninja Creami. Install the Creami paddle into the pint lid, attach the outer bowl, and lock it in place. Select the Lite Ice Cream mode and let it spin for several minutes.
4. Respin if necessary: After spinning, check the ice cream's consistency. If it's not creamy and smooth, and instead powdery, it needs to be respun. Return the pint container to the Ninja Creami and push the respin button. Repeat the process until a smooth texture is achieved.
5. Mix-in sugar-free chocolate chips: Once the ice cream is smooth, add the sugar-free chocolate chips. Create an indent in the center of the ice cream (there should already be a small one from spinning), and pour in the chocolate chips. Return it to the Ninja Creami and press the mix-in button to incorporate.
6. Finish and serve: When the mixing is complete, serve the ice cream immediately and enjoy!

## 54. NINJA CREAMI KEY LIME PIE ICE CREAM

Prep Time: 10 minutes

Cook Time: 5 minutes

Rest Time: 1 Day

Total Time: 1 day 15 minutes

Serving: 1

### Ingredients

- 1 tbsp Cream Cheese
- 1 cup of Whole Milk
- 3/4 cups of Heavy Cream
- 1/3 cup of Granulated Sugar
- 2 Graham Crackers
- 1 tsp Lime Extract
- 2 tbsp Key West Lime Juice (Can substitute lime juice)
- A few drops Green + Yellow Food Coloring (Optional)

### Instructions

1. Place 1 tbsp of cream cheese in a medium bowl and microwave it for 5-10 seconds to soften it up.
2. Add 1 tsp of lime extract and 1/3 cup of granulated sugar to the bowl with the cream cheese. Whisk the ingredients together until they are well mixed.
3. Slowly whisk in 1 cup of whole milk and 3/4 cup of heavy cream to the bowl with the cream cheese mixture.
4. Whisk in 2 tbsp of key west lime juice.
5. (Optional) Add a few drops of green and yellow food coloring and whisk until the mixture reaches the desired color.

6. Pour the mixture into a Ninja Creami pint container, ensuring that it does not go over the max fill line.
7. Freeze the pint for 24 hours, making sure it is placed on a flat surface in the freezer.
8. After 24 hours, remove the pint from the freezer and set up your Ninja Creami machine.
9. Remove the lid from the pint and place the pint securely into the outer bowl of the Ninja Creami machine. Cover the pint with the lid and place the outer bowl into the machine, twisting it to the right until it locks into place.
10. Press the "Ice Cream" button and wait for the ice cream to be ready.
11. Once the process is finished, press and hold the button on the left side of the Creami to twist the bowl to the left and remove it from the machine. Twist the lid off of the outer bowl and remove the pint.
12. Add the crushed graham crackers to the ice cream by carving a hole in the ice cream and dropping them in.
13. Place the pint back into the Ninja Creami machine and select the "Mix-In" button.
14. Enjoy your delicious homemade key lime pie ice cream!

## 55. NINJA CREAMI LEMON COOKIE ICE CREAM

Prep Time: 10 minutes

Cook Time: 5 minutes

Rest Time: 1 Day

Total Time: 15 minutes

Serving: 1

### Ingredients

- 1 tbsp Cream Cheese
- A Few Crushed Golden Oreos
- 1/3 cup of Granulated Sugar
- 3/4 cup of Heavy Cream
- 1 tsp Lemon Extract
- 1 cup of Whole Milk

### Instructions

1. To make this delicious lemon cookie ice cream, start by microwaving 1 tbsp of cream cheese in a medium bowl for 5-10 seconds to soften it up. Next, combine the cream cheese with 1 tsp of lemon extract and 1/3 cup of granulated sugar, and whisk until the ingredients are well mixed. Slowly whisk in 1 cup of whole milk and 3/4 cup of heavy cream, and then add a few drops of yellow food coloring until the mixture reaches the desired color.
2. Pour the mixture into a Ninja Creami pint container, taking care not to exceed the max fill line, and freeze the pint for 24 hours on a flat surface in the freezer. Once the freezing process is complete, remove the pint from the freezer and plug in your Ninja Creami machine.
3. Remove the lid from the pint and securely place the pint into the outer bowl of the Creami machine. Cover with the lid and lock the outer bowl into the machine by twisting it to the right until it clicks into place. Press the "Ice Cream" button and wait patiently for the magic to happen.
4. Once the ice cream is ready, press and hold the button on the left side of the Creami to twist the bowl to the left and remove it from the machine. Twist the lid off the outer bowl and remove the pint. It's time to add some mix-ins! Simply carve a hole in the ice cream and add some crushed golden Oreos. Place the pint back into the Creami machine and select "Mix-In".
5. Your lemon cookie ice cream is now ready to be enjoyed!

## 56. NINJA CREAMI MEXICAN HOT CHOCOLATE ICE CREAM

Prep Time: 10 Mins

Freeze Time : 1 Day

Cook Time: 5 Mins

Total Time: 1 Day 15 Mins

Serving: 4

### Ingredients

- 1/4 tsp Chili Powder
- 1/4 tsp Ground Cinnamon
- 2 tbsp Unsweetened Cocoa Powder
- 1 tsp Vanilla Extract
- 1 tbsp Cream Cheese
- 1 cup of Whole Milk
- 3/4 cup of Heavy Cream
- 1/3 cup of Granulated Sugar

### Instructions

1. 1.To make Mexican hot chocolate ice cream, start by softening 1 tbsp of cream cheese in the microwave for 5-10 seconds. Then, mix in 1 tsp of vanilla extract, 1/3 cup of granulated sugar, and 2 tbsp of unsweetened cocoa powder. Add 1/4 tsp of ground cinnamon and 1/4 tsp of chili powder, or 1/8 tsp each of chili powder and ground cayenne pepper for extra spice. Gradually stir in 1 cup of whole milk and 3/4 cup of heavy cream.
2. 2.Next, pour the mixture into a Ninja Creami pint container, making sure not to exceed the maximum fill line. Freeze the container on a flat surface in the freezer for 24 hours.
3. 3.After 24 hours, remove the pint from the freezer and place it in the Ninja Creami machine. Attach the outer bowl securely and cover it with the lid. Twist the outer bowl into the machine until it locks into place, then press the "Ice Cream" button and wait for the ice cream to be made.
4. 4.When the process is complete, hold down the button on the left side of the Creami to twist the bowl to the left and remove it from the machine. Take off the lid and remove the pint.
5. 5.Your Mexican hot chocolate ice cream is now ready to enjoy!

## 57. NINJA CREAMI MINT CHOCOLATE CHIP ICE CREAM

Prep Time: 10 Minutes

Rest Time: 1 Day

Total Time: 1 Day 10 Minutes

### *Ingredients*

- 1 cup of whole milk
- 4-6 drops green food coloring (optional)
- 1/4 cup of mini chocolate chips or finely chopped chocolate
- 1/3 cup of sugar
- 1 TBSP (1/2 ounce) cream cheese
- 3/4 cup of heavy cream
- 1 tsp peppermint extract

### *Instructions*

1. start by adding 1 tbsp of cream cheese to a microwave-safe bowl and microwaving it for 10 seconds until softened. Next, add 1/3 cup of granulated sugar and 1 tsp of peppermint extract to the bowl with the cream cheese, and use a silicone spatula or wooden spoon to mix them together until they form a thick paste.
2. In a separate measuring cup of of, combine 1 cup of whole milk and 3/4 cup of heavy cream. Gradually add this liquid to the sugar mixture, mixing well to combine. Start by adding a couple of tbsp at a time, and continue until all the liquid is added and the sugar has dissolved.
3. If desired, add a few drops of food coloring to the mixture and stir well to combine. Then, pour the mixture into a Ninja Creami pint, making sure not to exceed the max fill line. Close the lid and freeze the pint on a level surface in the freezer for 24 hours.
4. After 24 hours, remove the pint from the freezer and take off the lid. Add the pint to the bowl of the Ninja Creami and secure the lid. Insert the bowl into the machine and lock it into place. Select the Ice Cream function, which will run for about 2 minutes.
5. After spinning the ice cream, create a 1.5-inch well and add chocolate chips. Reinsert the bowl and use Mix In function to blend the chips. Serve and enjoy the peppermint chocolate chip ice cream!

## 58. MULLED APPLE CIDER ICE CREAM

Prep Time: 12 Minutes

Freeze Time: 1 Day

Total Time: 1 Day 12 Minutes

Serving: 1 Pint

### Ingredients

- 1 tsp + 1/4 tsp ground cinnamon, divided
- 1/2 tbsp butter for topping
- One tsp of vanilla extract
- 1/2 cup of Mott's® Apple Cider
- 1/2 cup of granny smith apple Slice
- Two tsp of orange zest
- Pinch of ground nutmeg
- 1/3 cup of light brown sugar
- Pinch of ground cloves
- 1 cup of heavy cream
- 1/2 cup of whole milk
- Pinch of ground allspice

### Instruction

1. In a large bowl, whisk together cream, whole milk, Mott's® Apple Cider, vanilla extract, brown sugar, 1 tsp cinnamon, nutmeg, allspice, cloves, and orange zest until evenly combined.
2. Pour the mixture into an empty CREAMi™ storage pint container and cover it with the storage lid. Freeze for 24 hours.
3. To make the apple topping, melt butter in a small saucepan over medium heat. Add apples and the remaining 1 tsp of cinnamon. Cook the apples in the

saucepan over medium heat, occasionally stirring, until they are soft and have a light brown color, which should take about 7-8 minutes. Transfer to a bowl and refrigerate until the ice cream is processed.
4. Remove the lid from the pint and take it out of the freezer.
5. Place the pint into the outer bowl of the Ninja Creami and attach the Creamerizer™ Paddle onto the outer bowl lid. Lock the lid assembly onto the outer bowl and put the bowl onto the motor base. Twist the handle to the right to raise the platform and lock it in place.
6. Select the "ICE CREAM" option.
7. Once the processing is complete, remove the ice cream from the pint and add the cinnamon apples on top.
8. Serve and enjoy!

## 59. ORANGE CREAMSICLE ICE CREAM

Prep Time: 15 Minutes

Freeze Time: 1 Day

Total Time: 1 Day 15 Minutes

Serving: 1

### *Ingredients*

- 1/2 tsp Vanilla Extract
- 1/3 cup of Granulated Sugar
- 1 tbsp Cream Cheese
- 1 cup of Whole Milk
- 3/4 cup of Heavy Cream
- 1 tsp Orange Extract
- A Few drops of Yellow + Red Food Coloring (Optional)

### *Instruction*

1. Place 1 tbsp cream cheese in a medium bowl and microwave for 5-10 seconds to soften it up.
2. Add 1 tsp orange extract, 1/2 tsp vanilla extract, and 1/3 cup of granulated sugar to the softened cream cheese. Whisk until the ingredients are well combined.
3. Slowly whisk in 1 cup of whole milk and 3/4 cup of heavy cream.
4. Add a few drops of yellow food coloring and a few drops of red food coloring to the mixture until you reach the desired orange color.
5. Pour the mixture into a pint-sized container designed for the Ninja Creami, being careful not to exceed the maximum fill line.
6. Freeze the pint for 24 hours on a flat surface in the freezer.
7. After 24 hours, remove the pint from the freezer and plug in your Ninja Creami machine.
8. Remove the lid from the pint container.
9. Securely place the pint container into the outer bowl of the Ninja Creami machine.
10. Cover the pint with the lid and twist the outer bowl into the machine until it locks into place.
11. Press the "Ice Cream" button and wait for the magic to happen.
12. Once the process is finished, press and hold the button on the left side of the Creami to twist the bowl to the left and remove it from the machine.
13. Twist the lid off of the outer bowl and remove the pint. Enjoy!

# 60. PEACH COBBLER FROUNCEEN YOGURT

Prep Time: 5 Minutes

Freeze Time: 1 Day

Total Time:1 Day 5 Minutes

Serving: 4

## Ingredients

- ¼ Tsp Cinnamon (Ground)
- ½ Tsp Vanilla Bean Paste (or Vanilla Extract)
- ¼ Cup of Honey Bunches of Oats-Just the Bunches
- 1 Tsp Sugar (White or brown)
- 12 Ounces Peach Yogurt (Noosa- with the fruit on the bottom)
- 15.5 Ounces Peaches (Canned- Slices in heavy syrup- Drain almost all of the syrup)

## Instruction

1. To make the frounceen yogurt, start by pouring the yogurt, half of the peaches (without the syrup), vanilla bean paste, cinnamon, and sugar into a Ninja Creami Pint. Stir the mixture until all the ingredients are well combined. Freeze the mixture on a level surface in a cold freezer for a full 24 hours.
2. After 24 hours, remove the pint from the freezer and take off the lid. Place the Ninja Creami pint into the outer bowl and put the outer bowl with the pint in it into the Ninja Creami machine. Turn the bowl until it locks into place. Press the LITE ICE CREAM button to start the function. The yogurt will mix together and become creamy during this process, which should take approximately 2 minutes.
3. Once the LITE ICE CREAM function is finished, turn the outer bowl and release it from the Ninja Creami machine.
4. If the frounceen yogurt appears dry and crumbly, do not worry. Dig a hole down the center of the frounceen yogurt and pour in the remaining peaches (without the syrup) and Honey Bunches of Oats. If necessary, add a tsp of milk to help moisten the mixture.
5. Next, place the Ninja Creami pint back into the outer bowl and put the outer bowl with the pint in it into the Ninja Creami machine. Turn the bowl until it locks into place, and then press the "MIX INS" button to start the process.
6. Your frounceen yogurt is now ready to eat! Enjoy it right away.

## 61. NINJA CREAMI PEACH ICE CREAM

Prep Time: 10 Minutes

Cook Time: 5 Mins

Freeze Time: 1 Day

Total Time: 1 Day 15 Minutes

Serving: 1

### Ingredients

- 3/4 cups of Heavy Cream
- 1 cup of Whole Milk
- 1/2 tsp Vanilla Extract
- 1 tbsp Cream Cheese
- 1/3 cup of Granulated Sugar
- 2/3 cups of Pureed Peaches

### Instruction

1. To make peach ice cream, start by softening 1 tbsp cream cheese in a medium bowl in the microwave for 5-10 seconds. Then add 1/2 tsp vanilla extract and 1/3 cup of granulated sugar, whisking until the ingredients are combined. Next, puree 2 peeled and cored peaches in a food processor, and whisk 2/3 cup of the puree into the cream cheese mixture. Slowly whisk in 1 cup of whole milk and 3/4 cup of heavy cream. Pour the mixture into a pint-sized container designed for the Ninja Creami, being careful not to exceed the maximum fill line, and freeze for 24 hours on a flat surface in the freezer.
2. After 24 hours, remove the pint from the freezer and place it in the Ninja Creami machine. Secure the pint in the outer bowl, cover it with the lid, and twist it to lock it into place. Press the "Ice Cream" button and wait patiently for the ice cream to be ready. Once done, twist the bowl to the left to remove it from the machine and remove the pint from the outer bowl.
3. If the ice cream is too hard, let it sit at room temperature for a few minutes to soften. Serve and enjoy your delicious peach ice cream!

## 62. APPLE PIE ICE CREAM

Prep Time: 5 minutes

Cook Time: 2 minutes

Additional Time: 1 day

Total Time: 1 day 7 minutes

Serving: 1 pint

### *Ingredients*

- 1 cup of canned apple pie filling
- 1/2 cup of heavy cream
- 1 tbsp (1/2 ounce) of cream cheese
- 1/4 cup of whole milk
- 2 tbsp of brown sugar
- 3/4 tsp of apple pie spice
- Optional: 1/4-1/2 cup of chopped graham crackers

### *Instructions*

1. Place the cream cheese in a large microwave-safe bowl and microwave it for 10 seconds to soften it.
2. Add the brown sugar and apple pie spice to the cream cheese and stir with a spatula or wooden spoon to create a thick paste.
3. In a separate bowl or large liquid measuring cup of, combine the heavy cream, milk, and apple pie filling. Use an immersion blender to pulse a few times and chop the apples into small pieces. Alternatively, you can chop the apples by hand before mixing them into the cream and milk.
4. Gradually add the liquid mixture to the sugar mixture, starting with a few tbsp at first. Whisk the mixture together until well combined, then continue adding liquid until all of it is incorporated.

5. Pour the mixture into a pint-sized container, like the Ninja Creami pint, and seal the lid. Put the container on a level surface in your freezer and let it freeze for 24 hours.
6. After 24 hours, take the container out of the freezer and remove the lid. Place the container in the outer bowl of the Ninja Creami and secure the outer bowl lid.
7. Transfer the outer bowl apparatus to the Ninja Creami machine. Press the ice cream button and allow the cycle to run for about 2 minutes.
8. Once the cycle is done, remove the bowl from the machine. Check the ice cream's texture and complete the Re-spin cycle if needed (see notes below).
9. To add mix-ins, create a 1/2-inch wide well in the ice cream that extends to the bottom of the container. Add 1/4 cup of chopped graham crackers to the well and run the container through the Mix-in cycle. Alternatively, you can top each serving of ice cream with chopped graham crackers.

**Notes:** If the ice cream isn't at your desired texture after the first cycle, complete the Re-spin cycle by putting the container back into the freezer for 1-2 hours before repeating the ice cream cycle.

## 63. BANANA ICE CREAM

Prep Time: 8 minutes

Freeze Time: 1 day

Total Time: 1 day 8 minutes

Serving: 4 pint

### Ingredients

- 1 tsp of banana extract
- 1 1/2 cup of overripe bananas, peeled and sliced
- 3 tbsp monk fruit sweetener*
- 1 cup of coconut cream

### Instructions

1. Begin by whisking the coconut cream until it's smooth.
2. Add the sliced bananas and lightly mash them with a fork.
3. Mix in the monk fruit sweetener and banana extract, stirring until the sweetener has dissolved.
4. Pour the mixture into a CREAMi pint, being careful not to go over the MAX FILL line. Put the lid on the pint and freeze it for 24 hours.
5. Remove the pint from the freezer and place it in the outer bowl. Attach the paddle and lid to the outer bowl.
6. Plug in the Ninja CREAMi unit and install the bowl on the base. Select LITE ICE CREAM and let it run until it shuts off.
7. Remove the bowl and lid from the pint. If the ice cream is too crumbly, reattach the lid and run the unit again with the RE-SPIN setting.
8. Once the ice cream is at the right consistency, serve immediately.

## 64. BANANA SWEET CREAM ICE CREAM

Prep Time: 5 minutes

Freeze Time: 1 day

Total Time: 1 day 5 minutes

Serving: 1 pint

### Ingredients

- 1/2 cups of whole milk
- 1/2 cups of weet cream-flavored coffee creamer
- 1 tsp vanilla bean paste
- 2-3 ripe bananas, cut into 1-2 inch chunks
- Optional: 1 tbsp milk

### Instructions

1. Combine the bananas, milk, coffee creamer, and vanilla bean paste in a blender. Blend for a few seconds until the ingredients are well combined.
2. Pour the mixture into a Ninja Creami pint container and place it on a level surface in the freezer for 24 hours.
3. After 24 hours, remove the pint from the freezer and take off the lid.
4. Place the pint in the outer bowl of the Ninja Creami machine and lock it into place. Press the ICE CREAM button.
5. During the ice cream function, the mixture will become creamy and smooth.
6. Once the ice cream function has ended, remove the pint container from the machine. If the ice cream is too dry and crumbly, add 1 tbsp of milk and re-spin once.
7. Turn the outer bowl to release it from the Ninja Creami machine.
8. Serve the ice cream, and enjoy!

## 65. NINJA CREAMI SALTED CARAMEL ICE CREAM

Prep Time: 10 minutes

Cook Time: 1 Day 10 Mins

Total Time:

Serving: 1

### Ingredients

- 3/4 cups of Heavy Cream
- 1 tbsp Cream Cheese
- 2 tbsp Caramel Dip
- 1 tsp Vanilla Extract
- 1/3 cup of Granulated Sugar
- 1 cup of Whole Milk
- 1/2 tsp Salt

### Instructions

1. To start making your Bourbon Salted Caramel Ice Cream, place 1 tbsp of cream cheese in a medium-sized bowl and microwave it for 5 to 10 seconds to soften it. This will make it easier to mix with the other ingredients.
2. Next, combine the cream cheese with 1 tsp of vanilla extract and 1/3 cup of granulated sugar. Whisk the mixture until everything is well combined.
3. Gradually whisk in 1/2 tsp of salt, 1 cup of whole milk, and 3/4 cup of heavy cream into the bowl with the cream cheese mixture.
4. In a separate small bowl, microwave 2 tbsp of caramel dip for 10 to 15 seconds until it's soft and easy to mix.
5. Whisk the caramel dip into the cream cheese mixture until it's fully incorporated and there are no lumps.

6. Pour the ice cream mixture into a Ninja Creami pint container, taking care not to fill it above the max fill line.
7. Freeze the pint for 24 hours on a flat surface in the freezer.
8. After 24 hours, take the pint out of the freezer and plug in your Ninja Creami machine. Place the pint securely into the outer bowl of the machine and cover it with the lid. Lock the outer bowl into place by twisting it to the right.
9. Press the "Ice Cream" button and wait patiently for the machine to finish making your creamy treat.
10. Once the process is complete, twist the outer bowl to the left using the button on the left side of the Creami to remove it from the machine. Twist off the lid of the outer bowl and remove the pint.
11. Now your delicious Bourbon Salted Caramel Ice Cream is ready to enjoy!

## 66. CARAMEL MOCHA OREO CRUMBLE ICE CREAM

Prep Time: 1 minute

Freeze Time: 1 day

Total Time: 1 day 1 minute

Serving: 1 pint

### Ingredients

- ¾ Cup of Caramel Almond Creamer
- 4 crushed Oreos
- 1 Cup of Chocolate Milk
- 6 Tbsp Coffee Syrup

### Instructions

1. Combine the chocolate milk and coffee syrup in a Ninja Creami pint and mix them together.
2. Fill the rest of the container with the caramel creamer.
3. Cover the container and freeze it for 24 hours.
4. After 24 hours, take the pint out of the freezer and place it into the outer bowl, then into the Ninja Creami machine. Choose the ICE CREAM process.
5. Once the process is complete, remove the ice cream from the machine and remove the lid.
6. Using a spoon, create a 1.5-inch hole down the middle of the ice cream and add in 3 of the crushed Oreos.
7. Put the lid back onto the pint and place it back into the outer bowl of the Ninja Creami machine. Choose the MIX IN setting.
8. Scoop the ice cream into a bowl and top it with the remaining crushed Oreo. Enjoy your delicious ice cream!

## 67. CHOCOLATE ICE CREAM

Prep Time: 5 minutes

Additional Time: 1 day

Total Time: 1 day 5 minutes

Serving: 1 pint

### Ingredients

- 1/3 cup of sugar
- 2 tbsp of cocoa powder
- 1 cup of whole milk
- 1 1/2 tsp of vanilla extract
- 1 tbsp of cream cheese (1/2 ounce)
- 3/4 cup of heavy whipping cream

### Instructions

1. Microwave the cream cheese in a microwave-safe bowl for 10 seconds.
2. Add the sugar, vanilla extract, and cocoa powder to the cream cheese and mix well with a silicone spatula or wooden spoon until thick paste forms.
3. In a separate measuring cup of, combine the whole milk and heavy cream. Gradually add this liquid to the sugar mixture, stirring well after each addition until all the liquid is added and the sugar has dissolved.
4. Pour the mixture into a pint-sized container that is compatible with the Ninja Creami. Close the lid and freeze it on a level surface in your freezer for 24 hours.
5. After 24 hours, remove the container from the freezer and remove the lid. Add the container to the bowl of the Ninja Creami and secure the lid. Insert the bowl into the machine and lock it into place.
6. Select the Ice Cream function, which will run for approximately 2 minutes.
7. Once the function is complete, unlock the bowl and remove the lid. Serve and enjoy your delicious homemade ice cream!

## 68. CINNAMON SPICE FROUNCEEN YOGURT-LITE ICE CREAM

Prep Time: 10 minutes

Freeze Time: 1 day

Total Time: 1 day 10 minutes

Serving: 1 pint

### Ingredients

1. 1/2 cup of nonfat Greek yogurt
2. 1/8 cup of allulose
3. 1 tsp of sugar-free Torani Vanilla syrup
4. 1 cup of Harney & Sons Hot Cinnamon Spice tea (brewed)

### Instructions

1. Combine all of the ingredients in a Creami pint container.
2. Add the pint container to the outer bowl and insert it into the machine.
3. Spin the ingredients together using the "milkshake" setting.
4. Remove the pint container from the outer bowl and freeze it for 24 hours.
5. After 24 hours, take the pint container out of the freezer.
6. Add the pint container to the outer bowl and insert it into the machine.
7. Choose the "Lite ice cream" setting and process the mixture.
8. If the texture and consistency of the ice cream are not to your liking, you can respin it once or twice.
9. Enjoy your delicious homemade ice cream!

**Note:** This recipe features the warming and spicy Harney & Sons Hot Cinnamon Spice tea paired with creamy Greek yogurt, sugar-free vanilla syrup, and allulose for sweetness. It's a guilt-free way to enjoy a tasty treat!

## 69. COCONUT LIME ICE CREAM

Prep Time: 10 minutes

Total Time: 10 minutes

Serving: 1 pint

### Ingredients

- 1 tbsp of lime zest
- 1/2 cup of freshly squeezed lime juice (about 5 limes)
- 1/4 cup of water
- 1 can (13.66 ounces) of coconut milk
- 1 cup of Grade A maple syrup, or to taste
- 2 avocados, peeled and pitted

### Instructions

1. Merge all ingredients in a blender or food processor, blending until a uniform texture is attained.
2. Scrape down the sides of the blender or food processor a few times to ensure a smooth texture. A blender is recommended for the smoothest texture.
3. Pour the mixture into an ice cream maker and freeze it according to the manufacturer's instructions.
4. This will typically take about 20 minutes or until the ice cream can be scooped without sliding off the spoon right away.
5. Serve immediately for a soft-serve texture, or freeze for a firmer texture.
6. If the ice cream is too hard after freezing, let it soften on the counter for about 15 minutes before serving.

## 70. COFFEE ICE CREAM

Prep Time: 8 minutes

Freeze Time: 1 day

Total Time: 1 day 8 minutes

Serving: 4

### *Ingredients*

- 2 Tbsp raw agave nectar
- 1 cup of unsweetened almond milk
- 1 1/2 Tbsp instant coffee
- 3 Tbsp monk fruit sweetener
- 1 tsp vanilla extract
- 3/4 cups of heavy cream

### *Instructions*

- In a mixing bowl, stir together all ingredients until sweetener and instant coffee are dissolved, creating the ice cream base.
- Pour the base into the CREAMi pint, ensuring it doesn't exceed the MAX FILL line, and then put on the lid.
- Place the pint in the freezer, ensuring it's level, and freeze for 24 hours.
- Remove the pint from the freezer, take off the lid, and place it in the outer bowl. Attach the paddle to the lid and install the lid onto the outer bowl.
- Plug in the Ninja CREAMi unit and install the bowl on the base.
- Select LITE ICE CREAM and press the power button. Wait until the unit shuts off.
- Remove the bowl from the base and take off the lid.
- If the ice cream is too crumbly, reattach the lid and install the bowl on the base again. Select RE-SPIN.
- Once the ice cream has the desired consistency, serve immediately.

## 71. DAIRY-FREE PUMPKIN ICE CREAM

Prep Time: 10 minutes

Freeze Time: 1 day

Total Time: 1 day 10 minutes

Serving: 1 pint

### *Ingredients*

- 1 tbsp cream cheese, room temperature or microwave for 10-20 seconds
- 1/4 cup ofmilk
- 1 1/4 cups of full-fat coconut milk, warmed and cooled to room temperature
- 1/2 tsp of cinnamon
- 1 tbsp of rum
- 1/2 cup of packed brown sugar
- 2 tsp of pure vanilla paste or extract
- 1/4 tsp of ground nutmeg
- 1/2 cup of canned pumpkin purée
- Optional: 1/8 tsp of xanthan gum

### *Instructions*

1. Combine the coconut milk, pumpkin, brown sugar, rum, vanilla paste, cinnamon, and nutmeg in a blender jar.
2. Blend the mixture until it is smooth.
3. If you're using xanthan gum, add it through the hole in the top of the blender while it's blending on low. Then, replace the top and blend on high for 15 seconds.
4. Pour the mixture into the container of your ice cream maker (such as a Ninja Creami) and freeze it for 24 hours.
5. If you're using a different ice cream maker, add the mixture to the machine and freeze it according to the manufacturer's instructions.

## 72. FROUNCEEN YOGURT ICE CREAM

Prep Time: 2 minutes

Cook Time: 2 minutes

Freeze Time: 1 day

Total Time: 1 day 4 minutes

Serving: 1 pint

### Ingredients

- 16 ounces of yogurt of your choice
- Optional: 1 tbsp of milk

### Instructions

1. Take a Ninja Creami pint container and add the yogurt to it. Use a spoon to press it down firmly, making sure to eliminate any air pockets. Then, close the lid on the container.
2. Transfer the container to a flat surface in your freezer and let it freeze for 24 hours.
3. When ready, remove the container from the freezer and take off the lid. Place the pint container into the outer bowl of the Ninja Creami, making sure to secure the outer bowl lid into place.
4. Put the outer bowl into the Ninja Creami machine and lock it into place.
5. Select the Lite Ice Cream button and let the cycle run for about 2 minutes.
6. If the mixture is crumbly after spinning, add a tbsp of milk and run it through a Re-spin cycle.
7. Finally, enjoy your homemade yogurt ice cream!

## 73. PISTACHIO ICE *CREAM*

Prep Time: 10 minutes

Cook Time: 5 minutes

Freeze Time: 1 day

Total Time: 1 day 15 minutes

Serving: 1 pint

### *Ingredients*

- 1 1/2 cups of whole milk
- 1/2 cup of heavy whipping cream
- 3.4-ounce box of instant pistachio pudding mix (amount may vary)
- Optional: 1/4 cup ofchopped pistachios

### *Instructions*

1. To make the ice cream, whisk together the instant pistachio pudding mix (the amount used may vary based on preference), whole milk, and heavy whipping cream in a medium mixing bowl.
2. Continue whisking for about 2 minutes until the pudding mix is dissolved and the mixture thickens slightly.
3. Next, pour the mixture into a Ninja Creami pint and close the lid. Place the pint on a level surface in the freezer and let it freeze for 24 hours.
4. After the freezing time is up, remove the pint from the freezer and take off the lid. Insert it into the Ninja Creami bowl and secure the lid. Lock the bowl into the machine.
5. Choose the Ice Cream function on the machine, which will run for about 2 minutes.
6. Once the cycle is complete, remove the pint from the machine.
7. If desired, make a well in the center of the ice cream that extends to the bottom of the pint and is about 1 1/2 inches wide.
8. Add chopped pistachios to the well.
9. Then, return the bowl with the pint to the machine and use the Mix In function to incorporate the pistachios.

## 74. PROTEIN ICE CREAM

Prep Time: 1 day

Cook Time: 10 minutes

Freeze Time: 1 day

Total Time: 1 day 10 minutes

Serving: 1 pint

### Ingredients

- 1 bottle (11.5 ounce) of Fairlife Protein Shake in any flavor
- Optional: mixins such as M&Ms, Oreos, etc.

### Instructions

1. Place the Fairlife protein shake into a pint container and let it freeze for 24 hours.
2. Once 24 hours have passed, take the pint out of the freezer and let it sit for 10 minutes to soften.
3. Next, place the pint into the Creami machine and set it to Sorbet mode. After running it on Sorbet, run it again on Respin mode.
4. Assess the consistency of the ice cream and determine if it matches your desired texture. If not, experiment with another respin or switch to Lite Ice Cream mode.
5. Assess the texture again and continue the respin process until it reaches the desired consistency.
6. If you prefer, add your desired mixins before serving.

## 75. PUMPKIN ICE CREAM

Prep Time: 5 minutes

Cook Time: 2 minutes

Freeze Time: 1 day

Total Time: 1 day 7 minutes

Serving: 1 pint

### Ingredients

- 1 cup of whole milk
- 1/2 tsp of vanilla extract
- 1 tbsp (1/2 ounce) of cream cheese
- 1/4 cup of pumpkin puree
- 3/4 cup of heavy cream
- 1 tsp of pumpkin pie spice
- 1/3 cup of packed light brown sugar

### Instructions

1. In a microwave-safe mixing bowl, microwave the cream cheese for 10 seconds to soften it.
2. Mix the brown sugar and pumpkin pie spice into the softened cream cheese using a spatula until a paste is formed.
3. Mix in the pumpkin puree and vanilla extract until fully incorporated.
4. Add the whole milk and heavy cream gradually to the paste, whisking in a few tbsp at a time until the mixture becomes smooth and all the liquid is well-incorporated.
5. Afterward, transfer the mixture into a Ninja Creami pint and ensure that the lid is securely closed. Then, place the pint onto a flat surface within the freezer and let it freeze for a full 24 hours.
6. Once the 24-hour period has elapsed, extract the pint from the freezer and take off its lid. Proceed to place the pint inside the outer bowl of the Ninja Creami and tightly secure the outer bowl lid.
7. Securely lock the outer bowl into position within the Ninja Creami machine, then select the Ice Cream button and allow the cycle to operate for roughly 2 minutes.
8. Upon completion of the cycle, remove the outer bowl from the machine. In the event that the ice cream is brittle, mix in a tbsp of milk, and utilize the Re-spin function to rotate the mixture once more. Now you can serve it right now

# NINJA CREAMI MILK SHAKE

## 76. VEGAN PEANUT BUTTER COOKIE MILKSHAKE

Prep Time: 5 Mins

Freeze Time: 1 Day

Total Time: 1 Day 5 mins

Serving: 1

### Ingredients

- ¼ Cup of Chocolate Chunks (or Chips)
- ½ Cup of Peanut Butter
- ¼ Cup of Half and Half

**Mix-Ins**

- 4-5 Bananas
- ¼ Cup of Cocoa Powder (Dark Cocoa Powder)

### Instruction

1. To prepare this recipe, start by putting some ice cream into an empty CREAMi™ Pint. Then, using a spoon, make a hole in the center of the ice cream that goes all the way to the bottom of the pint. Next, add the other ingredients to the hole.
2. Put the pint into an outer bowl and attach the Creamerizer™ Paddle to the lid of the outer bowl. Secure the lid assembly onto the outer bowl and place the bowl assembly onto the motor base. Turn the handle to the right to raise the platform and lock it in place.
3. Select the MILKSHAKE setting and wait for the processing to finish. Once done, remove the milkshake from the pint and serve it immediately.

# 77. NINJA CREAMI LOW CALORIE CHOCOLATE CHEESECAKE

Prep Time: 20 Mins

Cooking Time: 30 Mins

Total Time: 50 Mins

Serving: 4

## Ingredients

- 15 Milliliters Liquid Saccharine
- 6 Fat-Free Cheese Triangles
- 50 Milliliter Water (Hot)
- ¼ Tsp Xanthan Gum
- Water (Cold)
- 15 Grams Dark Cocoa Powder

## Instructions

1. Bloom the cocoa powder by stirring it into the hot water in the pint tub until it is completely dissolved.
2. Add the liquid saccharine or any sugar substitute to the pint tub and stir until well combined.
3. Add the unwrapped cheese triangles to the pint tub and blend until well combined using an immersion blender.
4. Add cold water up to the max line and blend in the xanthan gum.
5. Put the lid on the Ninja Creami Pint and freeze for 24 hours.
6. After 24 hours, remove the pint from the freezer and take off the lid. Place it into the Ninja Creami outer bowl.
7. Choose the "Smoothie Bowl" setting and process the ice cream according to the manufacturer's instructions.
8. Once the machine has finished processing, remove the pint from the outer bowl and serve immediately.

## 78. STRAWBERRY BANANA MILKSHAKE

Prep Time: 5 minutes

Total Time: 5 minutes

Serving: 1

### Ingredients

- 1/4 cup of banana slices
- 1 1/2 cups of keto-friendly strawberry ice cream from Ninja CREAMi
- 1/2 cup of unsweetened vanilla almond milk

### Instructions

1. Take a Ninja CREAMi pint container and place 1 1/2 cup of keto strawberry ice cream inside it.
2. Proceed to make a 1.5-inch hole in the center of the ice cream that goes all the way down to the bottom of the container.
3. Place the banana slices into the hole that you have created, and pour the unsweetened vanilla almond milk over them.
4. Put the pint container into the outer bowl, then attach the paddle to the lid and cover the outer bowl.
5. Connect the Ninja CREAMi unit to a power source and put the bowl onto the base.
6. Turn on the power button, and select the MILKSHAKE option.
7. Once the unit shuts off, remove the bowl from the base, and remove the lid.
8. Pour the milkshake into a cold glass, and top it with any desired toppings.
9. Serve the milkshake immediately.

## 79. THICK CHOCOLATE MILKSHAKE

Prep Time: 5 minutes

Total Time: 5 minutes

Serving: 1

### Ingredients

- 1/2 cup of Hood® Whole Milk
- 1 1/2 cup of chocolate ice cream

### Instructions

1. Take an empty CREAMi™ Pint and add all the ingredients in the order mentioned above.
2. Put the pint in the outer bowl, attach the Creamerizer™ Paddle onto the outer bowl lid, and secure the lid assembly onto the outer bowl.
3. Then, place the bowl assembly on the motor base and turn the handle to the right to raise the platform and lock it in place.
4. Select the MILKSHAKE option on the machine.
5. When the processing is complete, you can either add your desired mix-ins to the milkshake or remove the pint from the machine and serve it as is. Enjoy your delicious milkshake!

## 80. VANILLA MILKSHAKE

Prep Time: 5 minutes

Total Time: 5 minutes

Serving: 2

### Ingredients

- 1 cup of whole milk
- 2 cups of vanilla ice cream
- 1 tsp vanilla extract

### Instructions

1. Take a blender and add the vanilla ice cream, whole milk, and vanilla extract.
2. Blend all the ingredients together until they're well combined and you get a smooth and creamy mixture.
3. Pour the milkshake into glasses.
4. Serve the delicious vanilla milkshake immediately and enjoy!

## 81. DAIRY-FREE TAHINI CHOCOLATE COFFEE MILKSHAKE

Prep Time: 5 minutes

Total Time: 8 minutes

Serving: 1

### Ingredients

- 1/4 cup of tahini
- 1 tbsp vegan chocolate fudge
- 1/2 cup of unsweetened oat milk
- 1 1/2 cups of vegan chocolate ice cream
- 2 tbsp coffee

### Instructions

1. Put the vegan chocolate ice cream into an empty CREAMi™ Pint.
2. With the help of a spoon, create a hole in the pint that is 1 ½ inches wide and goes down to the bottom.
3. Next, add the unsweetened oat milk, tahini, coffee, and vegan chocolate fudge into the hole.
4. Put the pint into the outer bowl and attach the Creamerizer™ Paddle onto the lid of the outer bowl.
5. Securely lock the lid assembly onto the outer bowl. Then, place the bowl assembly on the motor base and turn the handle to the right in order to raise the platform and lock it firmly in place.
6. Choose the option for MILKSHAKE on the machine.
7. Once the processing is finished, take out the mouthwatering vegan chocolate milkshake from the pint and serve it promptly. Savor the delightful and revitalizing treat!

## 82. COFFEE AND CREAM MILKSHAKE

Prep Time: 5 minutes

Total Time: 5 minutes

Serving: 2

### Ingredients

- 1/2 cup of ice
- 4 Ninja® Single-Serve Scoops or 4 tbsp of ground coffee
- 2 cups of vanilla ice cream

### Instructions

1. Measure 4 scoops of ground coffee and place them into the brew basket.
2. Place 1/2 cup of ice in a large plastic cup of, and position the cup of in its place for brewing.
3. Choose the Travel Mug size and initiate the brewing process by pressing the Specialty Brew button.
4. Once the brewing is complete, combine the brewed coffee and ice with the vanilla ice cream in a blender container that is at least 24-ounces in capacity.
5. Blend the mixture until it is smooth, for about 25 seconds.
6. Divide the milkshake between 2 glasses and serve immediately.

## 83. ALMOND CANDY BAR MILKSHAKE

Prep Time: 5 minutes

Total Time: 5 minutes

Serving: 2

### Ingredients

- 2 tbsp of roasted, chopped almonds
- 2 tbsp of shredded coconut
- 1 1/2 cups of coco leche ice cream
- 2 tbsp of vegan chocolate chips
- 1/2 cup of almond milk

### Instructions

1. Put all the ingredients into an empty CREAMiTM Pint.
2. Next, put the pint in the outer bowl, attach the CreamerizerTM Paddle to the outer bowl lid, and lock the lid assembly on the outer bowl.
3. Then, place the bowl assembly on the motor base and twist the handle to the right to raise the platform and lock it in place.
4. Choose the MILKSHAKE setting on the appliance.
5. Once the blending process is finished, take out the milkshake from the pint and serve it promptly

# NINJA SMOOTHIE BOWLS

## 84. ALOHA TROPICAL SMOOTHIE BOWL

Prep Time: 5 minutes

Total Time: 5 minutes

Serving: 2

### Ingredients

- 1/3 cup of pineapple or apple juice
- 1 1/2 cups of ice
- 1 banana sliced
- 1 cup of strawberries quartered
- 1 cup of low-fat vanilla greek yogurt
- 1 cup of pineapple cubed

### Instructions

1. Place the cubed pineapple, quartered strawberries, sliced banana, low-fat vanilla Greek yogurt, ice, and pineapple or apple juice in a blender.
2. Puree the ingredients until the mixture is smooth and creamy.
3. If the consistency is too thick, add a little more pineapple or apple juice until it reaches the desired consistency.
4. Pour the smoothie into glasses and serve immediately.
5. Enjoy your delicious and healthy fruit smoothie!

## 85. BLUEBERRY MUFFIN SMOOTHIE BOWL

Prep Time: 5 minutes

Total Time: 5 minutes

Serving: 1

### Ingredients

- 1/2 tsp vanilla extract
- 1 cup of frounceen blueberries
- 1 fresh or frounceen banana
- 1/8 tsp fresh lemon zest (big pinch)
- 2 tbsp almond milk, or more as needed
- Toppings
- chia seeds or hemp seeds
- sliced almonds
- unsweetened coconut flakes
- fresh blueberries
- lemon slices
- almond butter or peanut butter
- 

### Instructions

1. Blend all smoothie ingredients in a high-speed blender, such as a Vitamix, until smooth. Add more almond milk as needed to achieve desired consistency.
2. Pour the smoothie into a bowl.
3. Add desired toppings, such as sliced almonds, almond or peanut butter, fresh blueberries, lemon slices, chia seeds or hemp seeds, and unsweetened coconut flakes.
4. Serve and enjoy your delicious smoothie bowl!

## 86. PITAYA PINEAPPLE SMOOTHIE BOWL

Prep Time: 5 minutes

Freeze Time: 1 day

Total Time: 1 day 5 minutes

Serving: 4

### Ingredients

- 12 ounces of pineapple juice
- 2 cups of frounceen pitaya (dragon fruit) chunks

**Toppings**

- Banana slices
- Seeds or nuts
- Mixed berries

### Instructions

1. Fill an empty CREAMi™ Pint to the MAX FILL line with frounceen pitaya chunks.
2. Pour pineapple juice over the pitaya chunks up to the MAX FILL line. Stir the pitaya and pineapple juice together, and add more juice if necessary to reach the max fill line. Put the storage lid on the pint and freeze for 24 hours.
3. Remove the pint from the freezer and the lid from the pint. Place the pint in the outer bowl, attach the CREAMi Paddle to the outer bowl lid, and lock the lid assembly onto the outer bowl. Place the bowl assembly onto the motor base and turn the handle to the right to raise the platform and lock it in place.
4. Select SMOOTHIE BOWL mode.
5. After processing is complete, transfer the smoothie to a bowl and garnish with desired toppings, such as banana slices, mixed berries, or seeds and nuts.

## 87. PINEAPPLE CUCUMBER SMOOTHIE BOWL

Prep Time: 5 minutes

Freeze Time: 1 day

Total Time: 1 day 5 minutes

Serving: 1

### *Ingredients*

1/4 cup of light coconut milk*

1/2 cup of filtered water

1/2 of a large, ripe, peeled, frounceen banana

1 heaping cup of cubed pineapple (if using frounceen, omit ice)

1 medium lime, zested and juiced

2-4 ice cubes

1 large handful of greens

1/2 cup of sliced cucumber

### *Instructions*

1. Add the cucumber, pineapple, frounceen banana, light coconut milk, water, lime zest, lime juice, greens, and ice cubes to a blender.
2. Blend the ingredients on high until the mixture is creamy and smooth. Be sure to scrape down the sides of the blender as needed.
3. For a thicker smoothie, add more ice. For a thinner smoothie, add more of your preferred liquid.
4. Taste the smoothie and adjust the flavors as needed. Add more lime juice or zest for brightness and acidity, more banana or pineapple for sweetness, more coconut milk for creaminess, or more greens for a more intense green color.
5. Serve the smoothie immediately. Although leftovers can be kept in the fridge for up to 24 hours, it is ideal to consume the smoothie when it is fresh.

# 88. WATERMELON SMOOTHIE BOWL

Prep Time: 5 minutes

Total Time: 5 minutes

Serving: 4

## *Ingredients*

- 2 tbsp hemp seeds (or chia seeds)
- 1 lime
- Sweetener of your choice
- 1 cup of frounceen strawberries
- 5 cups of fresh watermelon
- 1/2 cup of almond milk

## *Instructions*

Cut the watermelon into pieces and remove the seeds. Squeeze the lime juice into a bowl.

Place the watermelon chunks, frounceen strawberries, hemp seeds, almond milk, and sweetener into a blender.

Blend until smooth, making sure there are no chunks left.

If the smoothie is too thick, add more almond milk or water to thin it out.

Pour into glasses and enjoy your refreshing watermelon strawberry smoothie immediately!

## 89. GLOWING GREEN SMOOTHIE BOWL

Prep Time: 5 minutes

Total Time: 5 minutes

Serving: 2

### Ingredients

- 1 apple
- 1 1/2 cups of spinach
- 1/2 cup of coconut water
- 2 heads of romaine lettuce
- 1 pear
- 1 lemon, peeled
- 1 banana
- Optional: 1 serving of homemade protein powder

### Instructions

1. In a blender, add the spinach, romaine lettuce, peeled lemon, and coconut water.
2. Blend until the mixture is smooth, adding more water if necessary to reach desired consistency.
3. Add the pear, apple, banana, and protein powder (if using) to the blender.
4. Blend again until the mixture is smooth and creamy.
5. Pour the smoothie into a glass and enjoy the green goodness!

## 90. HEALTHY STRAWBERRY BANANA SMOOTHIE BOWL

Prep Time: 5 minutes

Cook Time: 0 minutes

Total Time: 5 minutes

Serving: 1

### Ingredients

- ½ Cup of Greek Yogurt (Nonfat)
- 1 Cup of Harney & Sons Hot Cinnamon Spice tea (Brewed)
- 1 Tsp Sugar-Free Torani Vanilla syrup
- ⅛ Cup of Allulose

### Instructions

1. Combine all ingredients in a Creami pint container and place it in the outer bowl of the ice cream maker.
2. Spin the mixture using the "milkshake" setting to mix the ingredients together. Then, remove the pint container from the outer bowl.
3. Freeze the pint container for 24 hours. After 24 hours, put the container back into the outer bowl and select the "Lite ice cream" setting to process the ice cream. If you're not satisfied with the texture and consistency, you can respin once or twice. Finally, enjoy your delicious homemade ice cream!

# 91. STRAWBERRY BANANA PROTEIN SMOOTHIE BOWL

Prep Time: 5 minutes

Rest Time: 1 Day

Total Time: 1 Day 5 minutes

Serving: 4

## Ingredients

- 1 cup of fresh raspberries
- 1/4 cup of vanilla yogurt
- 2 tbsp raw agave nectar
- 1 cup of fresh blackberries
- 1 cup of fresh strawberries, stems removed, quartered

## Instructions

1. To make this recipe, start by filling an empty CREAMi™ Pint up to the MAX FILL line with sliced bananas and strawberries. Mix the fruit until it's evenly distributed.
2. Next, in a large bowl, whisk together the remaining ingredients until they are well combined. Pour the mixture over the fruit in the pint up to the MAX FILL line and stir until everything is well combined. If needed, add more milk to reach the MAX FILL line. Cover the pint with the storage lid and freeze it for 24 hours.
3. After 24 hours, remove the pint from the freezer and take off the lid. Place the pint in an outer bowl and install the Creamerizer™ Paddle onto the outer bowl lid. Lock the lid assembly onto the outer bowl, then place the bowl assembly on the motor base and twist the handle right to raise the platform and lock it in place.
4. Select the SMOOTHIE BOWL setting on the motor base and let it process until complete. When done, transfer the mixture to a bowl and garnish with desired toppings. Enjoy!

## 92. NINJA CREMI RAZZLEBERRY SMOOTHIE BOWL

Prep Time: 5 minutes

Rest Time: 1 Day

Total Time: 1 Day 5 minutes

Serving: 1

### Ingredients

- 2 tbsp raw agave nectar
- 1 cup of fresh raspberries
- 1 cup of fresh strawberries, stems removed, quartered
- 1 cup of fresh blackberries
- 1/4 cup of vanilla yogurt

### Instructions

1. Combine all ingredients in a large bowl and whisk until well combined.
2. Pour the mixture into an empty CREAMi™ Pint. Place the storage lid on the pint and freeze it for 24 hours.
3. After 24 hours, remove the pint from the freezer and take off the storage lid. Place the pint in an outer bowl and install the Creamerizer™ Paddle onto the outer bowl lid. Lock the lid assembly onto the outer bowl, then place the bowl assembly on the motor base and twist the handle right to raise the platform and lock it in place.
4. Select the SMOOTHIE BOWL setting on the motor base.
5. Once the processing is complete, transfer the mixture to a bowl and garnish with your desired toppings. Enjoy!

## 93. BANANA PEANUT BUTTER OAT BOWL

Prep Time: 5 minutes

Total Time: 5 minutes

Serving: 1

### Ingredients

- 1/4 cup of rolled oats
- 1/2 cup of vanilla Greek yogurt
- 1/2 tsp cinnamon
- 1 frounceen banana, cut in quarters
- 1 tbsp creamy peanut butter

### Instructions

1. Place all of the ingredients in the 14-ounce Power Nutri Bowl in the order listed, then install the blade assembly.
2. Select the BOWL function on your blender, and twist the Power Paddle counterclockwise continuously while blending until the program is complete.
3. Once the blending is complete, remove the blade assembly from the Nutri Bowl.
4. Decorate your smoothie with your favorite toppings and serve it right away. Enjoy!

## 94. AVOCADO KALE SMOOTHIE BOWL

Prep Time: 5 minutes

Freeze Time: 1 Day

Total Time: 1 Day 5 minutes

Serving: 1

### Ingredients

- 1 banana, cut into 1-inch (2.5cm) pieces
- 1 cup of packed kale leaves
- 2 tbsp agave nectar
- 1 cup of green apple pieces, 1-inch (2.5 cm) each
- 1/4 cup of unsweetened coconut milk
- 1/2 avocado, cut into 1-inch (2.5cm) pieces
- Utensils
- Blender

### Instructions

1. Combine the banana, avocado, kale, apple, coconut milk, and agave in a blender. Blend on high for about 1 minute until the mixture is completely smooth.
2. Pour the blended mixture into a clean CREAMi™ Pint. Place the storage lid on the container and freeze it for 24 hours.
3. Remove the pint from the freezer and take off the lid. Place the pint in the outer bowl of your Ninja® CREAMi™ machine. Install the Creamerizer™ Paddle in the outer bowl lid and lock the lid assembly onto the outer bowl. Place the bowl assembly on the motor base, and twist the handle to the right to raise the platform and lock it in place.
4. Select the Smoothie Bowl function on your Ninja® CREAMi™ machine and let it process until finished.
5. Once the machine has finished processing, remove the smoothie bowl from the pint.
6. Serve the smoothie bowl immediately with your desired toppings. Enjoy!

# 95. NINJA CREAMI COFFEE SMOOTHIE BOWL

Prep Time: 5 minutes

Freeze Time: 1 Day

Total Time: 1 Day 5 minutes

Serving: 1

## Ingredients

**Smoothie Bowl**

- 2 Tbsp Mocha Almond Butter
- ½ Cup of Oat Milk
- 1 Cup of Coffee (Brewed- not just the coffee beans or grounds)
- 1 Banana
- 1 Cup of Raspberries

**Toppings**

- 1 Tsp Honey
- ½ Cup of Raspberries
- 1 Tbsp Sliced Almonds
- ¼ Cup of Chocolate Covered Espresso Beans
- 1 Banana
- Maple Syrup

*Instructions*

1. In a blender, combine all of the ingredients and blend until the mixture is smooth.
2. Pour the mixture into an empty pint container for the Ninja Creami machine and freeze it for 24 hours.
3. Once the mixture has frounceen for 24 hours, remove the pint container from the freezer and take off the lid.
4. Place the pint container into the outer bowl for the Ninja Creami machine and lock it in place by turning it.
5. Press the "Smoothie" button on the Ninja Creami machine to begin the blending process. Allow the machine to blend the mixture until it becomes very creamy.
6. After the smoothie function has ended, turn the outer bowl to release it from the Ninja Creami machine.
7. Scoop the smoothie into a bowl and drizzle it with maple syrup or honey. Top it with sliced almonds, chocolate-covered coffee beans, raspberries, and sliced bananas, or any other desired toppings.
8. Enjoy your delicious smoothie bowl!

# The End!

Printed in Great Britain
by Amazon

f2a702b6-63fb-4baf-bf33-bb4e36dc0a08R01